My Life Defined...

My Life Defined...

ISBN-13: 978-1500775179
ISBN-10: 1500775177
ASIN: B00MI5F13Q

Edited by Lorna Collins
Cover design by Melissa Summers
Cover collage by Pauline Crawford Crabb

My Life Defined...

by

Pauline Crawford Crabb

TABLE OF CONTENTS

Dedication i

Acknowledgements.. ii

Introduction... 1

Chapter 1 ...by the Irish Connection...................... 4

Chapter 2 ...by the Granite Mountains of Oregon 10

Chapter 3 ...by a Hard Rock Miner 26

Chapter 4 ...by a Miner's Wife 41

Chapter 5 ...by My Early Years............................ 51

Chapter 6 ...by Life on the Run 59

Chapter 7 ...by a Jail Cell.................................... 66

Chapter 8 ...by Santo Tomas Internment Camp... 68

Chapter 9 ...by Joan's Story 82

Chapter 10 ...by the Idaho Years 84

Chapter 11 ...by the Boy from Kansas 121

Chapter 12 ...by the Summer of '53.................... 130

Chapter 13 ...by Life on Campus Drive 137

Chapter 14 ...by a Year in Las Vegas 147

Chapter 15 ...by Life in Pasadena...................... 153

Chapter 16 ...by Tuscany Hills 202

Chapter 17 ...by the Spanish Village by the Sea 222

Chapter 18 ...by Friends 228

Chapter 19 ...by Faith....................................... 233

Chapter 20 ...by a Backward Glance 240

Chapter 21 ...I Returned 246

About the Author 271

Dedication

This collection of my life's memories is dedicated to:

- my parents, Paul Crawford and Catherine Ladd Crawford, who gave me love and a solid foundation for the adventures and challenges ahead
- my dear husband, Leon Dee Crabb, who walked with me for over forty years, and who helped me define the meaning of my life
- my children, Leon, Larry, and Mary, who have supported me as I adventure through the rest of my life
- my grandchildren, Jeffrey, Lindsay, Ryan, Hannah, Victoria, and Steven, each of whom I love very much
- my great-granddaughters, Ashlyn, Brooklyn, and Veda, as well as other great-grandchildren who have yet to make their way into this family, and who will live in a far different world than that in which their Great-granny Crabb grew up

Acknowledgements

John Donne wrote "No man is an island," and in that same vein, I know I would not have been able to tell my story without the assistance of many others. A few I can name, but there are others who have shared memories which have helped me describe those people, places and events about which I have written. To them I also give thanks.

I am most grateful to my mother, Catherine Crawford, for being a Saver, with a capital 'S.' Because she saved so many mementos of the past, I was able, if only partially, to paint a picture, not only of my ancestors, but especially of my early years in the Philippine Islands, including our time in Santo Tomas.

Had not Bill Moule written of his experiences in the Philippines during World War II, and Frederick Stevens not written a history of Santo Tomas, there might have been a gap in my narrative of how our family dealt with the hardships of those years. I am especially grateful to these two authors, and to others who also wrote and published their stories, which often brought to the surface some of my own recollections.

I'm not the first to say that writing can be a lonely experience. For too many years, more than I wish to acknowledge, I was reluctant to share my written words with others. As the chapters began to take shape, the artists in my painting critique group, Chris, Maureen, Carol, and Flossie, listened to bits and pieces of my story, and their enthusiasm encouraged me to keep writing. My friend, Patti Lynn, gave me the courage to include the chapter on my faith.

I am most thankful to another good friend, Kathy Schinhofen, for introducing me to author and editor, Lorna Collins, who graciously invited me to become a member of the Lagunita Writers' Group. Their keen insights into what makes a manuscript readable, their writing and publishing experiences, and their personal encouragement has given me the impetus to see this project through to the end.

I am especially grateful for Lorna's editing skills and advice, which have kept me glued to the computer, writing and re-writing, editing, and re-editing. With her help, my siblings, as well as my children, grandchildren, and great grandchildren will know something of their heritage.

Introduction

"There Was a Child Went Forth"
There was a child went forth every day;
And the first object he look'd upon,
that object he became;
And that object became part of him for the day,
or a certain part of the day, or for many years,
or stretching cycles of years.
Walt Whitman, *Leaves of Grass*

Walt Whitman's words have become like a beckoning finger as I try, now in my eightieth year, to recall those multitudes of objects, people, places and events I've looked upon over so many days and weeks and years. They are the *who,* the *what,* and the *where*, perhaps even the *why* that have defined my life. It has been an interesting journey traveling backward in time, using letters, photos, even, in this day of the internet, websites, trying to mesh together the pieces of my life like a thousand-piece jigsaw puzzle.

When we are young and in our prime, the past is often the least important component of our lives. We keep striving for new goals: at school, in our jobs and careers, for our families. And, sadly, many questions about our past become important only when the people who could give us answers have left this world. How many times do I wish I could ask my mother a question about my earlier life, or hers or my dad's, or my Granny Ladd's or Granny Scott's?

I hope that by putting to paper—or disk or thumb drive—a brief (or not so brief) accounting of my past, and present as well, my children, grandchildren, and whoever comes after them may have some idea of how I have defined my life.

Being the oldest of the five children of Paul and Catherine Crawford, I know each of us sees our family in a different light. Twenty-one years separate me and my youngest sibling. My memories do not necessarily coincide with hers, or any of the others for that matter. Years ago, when I taught parenting classes in Pasadena, quoting a now-forgotten expert, I used to say to the mothers in my classes, "No two children are ever born into the same family." The remark often brought furrowed brows. "The age of the parents, the economic circumstances, the number of children, health of the family..." I went on and on with examples, and they began to understand.

My own children and grandchildren each view me and one another from their own experiences, their own perspectives as well. The way I define my life may not mesh with the way they have defined my life, or will define it in the years to come. But I'm holding the pen, so to speak, and the words that flow into this story define my life as I have remembered it.

Finally, in my mind, the most important reason for wanting to write my story is because I want to acknowledge that I have been very blessed with not one but two loving families: the family into which I was born and grew up, and the family which, with my husband, I helped create. Life has always not always been perfect, nor all the people in it, but I have always felt loved. In the grand scheme of things, love is what matters most.

* * * * *

In 2015, I returned to the Philippines to attend the Seventieth Anniversary of the liberation of the Santo Tomas Internment Camp. I have added a chapter

My Life Defined...
describing the experience, as it brought my experience during the war full circle.

Chapter 1 ...by the Irish Connection

Mary Matilda Boyle and Hugh Maurice Crawford

During the summer of 2010, I had the privilege of going to Ireland on a watercolor painting workshop with Chris Van Winkle, with whom I'd traveled and painted many times before. It was not the first time I'd been to Ireland, and, as I had felt before, I had a deep sense of being connected to the land. Perhaps it's all in my head. Perhaps it's because my ancestry leads me there.

On one of our excursions to find a setting in which to set up our easels, we took in one of the tourist attractions in the village of New Ross, County Wexford. Anchored in the waterway known as 'The Quay' is a replica of the *Dunbrody*, a three-masted barque, identified as a 'famine ship' in history books. It transported emigrants from Ireland to Canada and America during the great potato famine in the mid-1840s. As we lined up along the gangplank leading onto the ship, we walked past a silver-colored plaque, a copy of a manifest of passengers who had made the often treacherous journey across the Atlantic Ocean in hopes

4

of finding sustenance in a new land. My eyes scanned the columns of names as I walked along. Suddenly, I cried out, "Oh my God, there's my grandfather's name – Hugh Crawford from Belfast."

I pointed the name out to my companions. They shared the news with some of the staff at the tourist center and I was an immediate celebrity. My fame lasted only for the next couple of days. An announcer from a local radio station even drove out to the artist's studio on her farm, where we were spending our days, to interview me, but that was about the extent of my time to shine.

In retrospect, it is unlikely that this Hugh Crawford, a passenger on the Dunbrody, was my paternal grandfather. It is more likely that he might have been my great-grandfather. I haven't had time to explore my lineage further, but it is a distinct possibility as genealogy records from the Mormon Church list my grandfather as Hugh Maurice Crawford, born in Canada in the year 1865, and being married on June 24, 1898. His parents are listed as Patrick Crawford and Ann Cirth, but no further personal information for him is listed. Who then was the Hugh Crawford, a passenger on the Dunbrody?

The same Mormon genealogy lists my father's mother as Mary Matilda Boyle, born October 4, 1882, in Elk Rapids, Michigan, where her parents, Michael Red Boyle and Clara M. Smith had been married. Another ancestry record, from a different source, lists her birth year as 1881. She was the oldest child, and only girl, with three younger brothers: Thomas, Charles, and Hugh. Both of Mary Matilda's paternal grandparents, Thomas H. Boyle, and Mary Margaret O'Donnell were born in Donegal, Ireland. Michael Red Boyle was their only child.

The census records of Germfask Township, Michigan in 1910, list the names of my grandfather, Hugh

Crawford, his wife, Mary M, (Mary Matilda, according to the Mormon genealogy) and four children, the youngest of whom is my father, Paul R., listed as five years old. This age isn't consistent with the information on my father's passport records which give his birth date as August 27, 1903.

On the census record, Hugh Crawford's occupation is listed as 'painter.' My mother told me that at one time he had been a Catholic seminarian. According to family members he was also an alcoholic and not a good father. In a note included in a Christmas card, in 1977, my Aunt Lillian wrote:

> *My mother, Mary Matilda, was just sixteen when she married Hugh Maurice Crawford. He was twenty years older than she. They had seven children: Clarence John, Lillian Marion, Glen Rexford, Paul (your father), Gail, who got a hold of some poison pills and passed at the age of three, Shirley, Maurice (who spells his name Morris). Our growing up years were not too happy. Paul was left in Manistique, Mich. when mother took the four younger children and moved to Montana. After a few years, we moved to Mullan, Idaho. I, Glen, and Paul went to high school in Mullan.*

From pictures in Mullan's town museum, Maurice also went to high school there, as he is pictured with a photograph of a basketball team. According to another cousin, she settled in Spokane, Washington, a city in the eastern part of the state where one or more of Mary Matilda's brothers were living. Here, the cousin tells me, she worked in a biscuit factory, and for a time, because she was having a hard time earning enough to feed all her family, placed her two youngest children in a Catholic orphanage.

Just when Paul rejoined the family, I don't know, but by 1917, when my father was fourteen years old, Matilda had moved her family to Mullan, a small town in the Idaho panhandle, where the children went to school, and where, as the boys grew older, they found work in the gold, lead and silver mines in the area. At some point during this time, Matilda met and married a second time. Her husband, Murray Scott, was a Canadian, who also worked in the mines in the area.

My first memories of Granny Scott, as we always called her, and of Murray, my step-grandfather, occur in 1945, the year our family returned from the Philippine Islands after World War II. At that time they were living on a 120 acre farm, in Careywood, Idaho, a rural community, located north of Mullan and Lake Coeur d'Alene, in Bonner County.

When I picture Granny Scott in my mind's eye, she is always wearing a full apron over a calico print dress. She is not very tall, but stands straight and is full-bodied. Her hair, reddish brown, is pulled back and tied at the nape of her neck. She has fair Irish skin, but weathered from working outside so many hours on the farm. Her arms are peppered with freckles. While I usually see her as stoic, I do have a photo in which she is smiling and wearing a decorative print scarf around her neck, and I think inside that stern composure is the heart of a young woman who has known love.

Murray was the only grandfather I ever knew. I never called him Granddad, only Murray. He was tall, stocky, and cheerful. He liked to tease me when we came to the farm in the summers while I was still in high school. One of the photos I have of him and 'Tilly,' as Murray always called my grandmother, reflects a happy couple.

Murray and Tilly eked out a living on the farm, which I once heard Granny call 'Scott's Bluff,' perhaps owing to the rocky soil, which made farming difficult. They planted two fields of grain, kept a cow or two, a horse named Dolly, as well as some hogs and chickens. Granny kept a thriving garden going. In 1945, when we first visited, there was still no electricity connected to the house, and an outhouse, down the hill from the barn, served as the family's bathroom. Maurice, Matilda's youngest son, lived on another small farm nearby and helped his mother and Murray.

Each summer, after our return to the States, my father would take all of his vacation time to go up to the ranch to help harvest the hay. Granny Scott and Murray lived on the farm until 1950, when she became ill and went to stay with her daughter, Lillian, in Portland, Oregon. Murray remained in on the farm in Careywood to take care of the property and their animals.

In the late 1940s, my parents had bought a farm (although we always called it 'the ranch') about a mile down the dirt road from where Granny lived. They rented the property to tenants while my father was still working at the Triumph Mine in southern Idaho. Our family moved to the ranch after I graduated from high school in 1950. I was at home that summer, when one day a messenger from the small combination store and post office down on the highway drove up with the news they had received a telephone call from my father's sister in Portland. We were to telephone Aunt Lillian as soon as possible. The messenger gave us the number to call. We didn't have a telephone at our house, and, for some reason which I can't remember, I was designated to take the jeep, our only motor vehicle other than a tractor, and drive down to the store to make the call. Details are faded, but I do remember giving the operator the number and hearing Aunt Lillian's voice tell me the sad news that my grandmother had had a stroke and died. I drove back to the ranch and parked the jeep by the house. From there I walked down the driveway and across a field to where my dad was plowing. It was so hard for me to tell my father that his mother had just died. I can still see him as he put his hand to his forehead, covered his eyes, and softly cried.

Sometime later that summer, after I had left for college, Aunt Lillian, brought her mother's ashes back to Careywood where they were scattered under an apple tree on the farm, next to the house where she had lived so many years. Some years later, Murray's and Aunt Shirley's ashes joined hers. And even later, in 1964, Daddy's ashes were spread with theirs.

The farm is still in the family. Half of the acres have been sold, but my cousin, Mary Ann Denning, the daughter of my father's youngest brother, Maurice, now lives in Granny Scott's house. The apple tree still grows in the yard.

Chapter 2 ...by the Granite Mountains of Oregon

Ella Mae Irwin and George LoRance Ladd

Many summers ago now, sometime after my mother's death, my siblings and I decided to hold a family reunion near my mother's birthplace: Cornucopia, in Baker County, Oregon. Since I was the only retired member of the five Crawford children, I offered to make the arrangements for our lodgings. Wanting to explore the roots of my mother's family, I decided to make a trip ahead of time, flew to Boise, Idaho, and rented a small car for the two to three hour drive, a distance of just under one hundred miles.

From Boise, on US Highway 84, I headed west and once I crossed the Snake River, I had left Idaho, and entered the state of Oregon. At Baker City, one of the stops along the old Oregon Trail, I turned off US 84, veering onto a two lane highway. The steep peaks of the well-named Granite Mountains came into view long before I had reached the small town of Halfway, nestled in the pristine Pine Valley. Twelve miles farther along a very narrow dirt road, at an altitude of eight thousand feet, lies Cornucopia, now a ghost town.

I had made reservations for two nights at the Cornucopia Lodge, and was pleasantly surprised, after a shaky drive up a rutty road, to find a newly built establishment, bounded by tall trees with a magnificent view of the Granites from every window of the building.

As I was registering, I remarked to the innkeeper, "I'm here because my mother was born in Cornucopia, and my grandfather was the Superintendent of the Last Chance Mine in the early 1900s. I'd like to explore a little tomorrow."

After a too-quiet night's sleep (I was the only guest that night, and it felt a little eerie), I woke early, got ready, and walked down to the dining room where a hearty breakfast was served to me at a table overlooking the jagged mountains in the distance. As I was enjoying the view, the wife of the proprietor came up to my table.

"Would you like me to show you the tunnel into the Last Chance?"

"Oh, that would be great." I was thrilled. What a bonus for me.

Soon we were walking along the dirt road that was once the main street of old Cornucopia. Now mainly abandoned, there remain only a few small wooden houses dotting the hillside. The old boarding house still stands, dilapidated with rotting timbers under its porches which are unprotected from the ravages of winter snows. From the front door, I peered inside and could see an old table and chairs still waiting for some old-timers to come in, sit down and swap stories of the ore they found, the cave-ins, the water problems, or the skunk in the outhouse. These men spent their lives miles underground: digging, dynamiting, picking the rock from quartz-bearing veins containing silver and gold, then

11

transporting the ore up from the depths of the earth on trams, dumping it out into sluices where it was washed, separating the chaff from the grain, so to speak, and finally hauling it to the mill.

A few minutes later we left the main road and took an overgrown trail up the hill a short distance. Without the innkeeper's wife guiding me, I would never have known how to reach the now boarded-up opening of the Coulter Tunnel where Rance Ladd, my grandfather, would have entered each day to get into the mine. Tall pines have obscured all but few glimpses of the tailings that poured out from the tram lines that brought the ore to the surface. I could see him hopping onto a tram, wearing a hard hat, rubber boots and coat to keep the dripping water from dampening his work clothes, getting himself ready for the day's or night's work ahead.

My companion left me to my thoughts, and with a sketchbook in my lap, I sat on a large stone by the small stream that ran in front of the tunnel, drawing and brushing watercolors onto a page, capturing a memory of the essence of that place and time. I was drawn back to the years when Cornucopia was a bustling community.

Gold may have been discovered in the Pine Valley of Oregon, as early as 1861, but by 1885, according to *1984 Pine Valley Echoes,* word had spread and "the rush came from all over the country and soon all the exposed mountainsides were staked off into mining claims and numerous multi-millionaires created overnight." The Last Chance Mine is said to have had "more rich pockets of gold than any of the others." Is it any wonder that my grandfather Rance's hopes and dreams of wealth lured him into this setting?

My mother's father was named George LoRance Ladd, but was always known as Rance Ladd. He was a native born Oregonian, born New Year's Day, 1879, in the then unincorporated community of Arlington, originally named Alkali, located in Gilliam County, whose northern border is the Columbia River. Rance's father, James Ladd, had been born in Illinois; his grandfather, James Lindsay Ladd was born in Kentucky and married a woman named Evangeline Slack, born in Iowa. When they migrated to Oregon I don't know. Rance had three sisters and no brothers. He was only twelve years old when his mother died. In one of his letters to my grandmother, Rance speaks of his father up on Red Mountain where Rance was working, so perhaps being a hard rock miner seemed a natural path to follow.

As with my paternal grandfather, there are no early photographs, no letters in childish handwriting, nothing to tell me about his day-to-day growing up. I only know of him as a suitor and future husband of my grandmother, Ella Mae Irwin, and as a man who spent most of his adult life pursuing the often elusive rich vein of gold.

Born in Nebraska on August 1, 1886, Ella Mae Irwin came with her parents, John and Mary Catherine Irwin, two brothers and two sisters, to Oregon as a young girl. Her father purchased property and eventually owned two farms in Carson, a small community adjacent to the town of Halfway, and only a few miles from Cornucopia where my mother, Catherine, would be born.

Just when Ella and Rance met is up to our imagination, but I have letters from one the other written two years before their marriage. Rance was twenty-six years old and Ella was nineteen, living at home with her parents. Rance was making his living as a miner. I imagine them meeting at Keller's Hall, or Chris Schneider's or Lincoln's, or a similar spot where one of the dances he often mentioned in his letters was held. Or perhaps he made himself known by offering to help with

13

the haying in the summertime on her parents' farm. He wrote about Ella's mother's cooking in one of the letters.

The earliest letter I have from Rance to Ella was written from Red Mountain, where his father had also worked. It was situated high on one of the Granite Peaks, reached from a road, which passed through Cornucopia. Several times Rance mentions a horse he owned, so I picture him astride a fairly lean animal, trudging his way up an unpaved road to the mine where he most probably lived in a boarding house.

On August 3, 1905, Rance wrote:

Dear Heart,

Henry [his brother-in-law?] *is going to town Saturday and while there is nothing to write still it may be the only chance I'll have to say "Hello" for a week and then you are rather particular about waiting to hear from me before you will write...*

I worked in the mine yesterday and today. Two days of the time I have to wait for you, gone. Henry is the cook and I can't say that I appreciate his cooking as much as I did yours and your Mamma's. Still there's no danger of my starving. H.S. of Eagle Valley is herding sheep in here and he spends most of his time with us. He went fishing today and caught 25 and brought them up to the mine. We will live high tomorrow morning...

After a few other inconsequential details about his life on the mountain, he writes:

...You have no idea how lonesome it is up here. I have got so used to being with you that if it was not for the end I have in view I wouldn't stay here at all. But if you don't change your mind "and I hope you will not" someday we will never have to part for I love you too well to be contented away from you.

My Life Defined...

I think I will write to Grace [his sister], *and tell her. She will be glad to know that I'm on the road to a more settled life and I'm sure that you two will be great friends if you ever become acquainted.*

The first night I was up here I dreamed of you and in my dream we were sweethearts. Heretofore whenever I saw you in a dream someone was taking you away from me.

It's almost bedtime and I've got to go in and shoot a hole in the tunnel before I go to sleep. This letter don't amount to much but it carries my love to you. Write to me and take pity upon a poor lonely old miner and tell me all that is going on and love me a great deal.

Regards to the folks. Love and kisses to Ella Sweetheart mine.

Your own

Geo. R. Ladd

The 'hole in the tunnel,' to which Rance referred, was made by placing a stick of dynamite strategically near a vein where the valuable ore was located, then detonating it. This was always done by the night shift (or, as I suspect in this case, a single person) so that in the morning, after the dust and rock had settled, the day shift would come in and load the ore into trams on its journey to the mill. Mining was, and is, a dangerous and unhealthy occupation.

For the next two years, between 1905 and 1907, Rance worked at a number of mines. He mentions the Tenderfoot Mine, Basic Mines, the Chief and Red Boy and 'Dr. Wilson's claims.' He writes, in 1906, about *"going up to Red Mountain today and work for Henry for a few days. I've been working up on the Jonathan Bourne claims and have made pretty good wages, $15.00 a day, but I had to cancel out and the day after I moved up I*

15

went over to the Robert Emmet and May Flower and it rained on me..."

As Mother told me, Rance was a very sociable fellow and had lots of friends. He sometimes played music (piano or fiddle) in a bar or saloon. I can see how Ella might have been attracted to him.

But also among the letters I found addressed to my grandmother, is one in a small blue, very faded envelope addressed to Miss Ella Irwin, Carson, Baker County, Ore. It is postmarked, not from Oregon but from Nevada. It was written on yellowed onion-skin lined paper. The penmanship style does not match that of my grandfather.

Good Springs, Nevada

March 27, 1907

Dear Miss Irwin,

There can be no more painful situation than that in which one is placed when being anxious to secure the affection of another, yet has not been able to discover whether there is a probability of success. I have for some time found myself in that situation. I am most anxious that you should give me some return of the feeling with which I regard you, and I am quite without any knowledge as to whether you look upon me with favor or not. May I take the liberty, if it be one of solving my doubt by the straightforward process of direct avowal of my love, and as straightforward a question as to how I am estimated by yourself? Nothing is worse than suspense. I would know the truth, and even bear its being the reverse of agreeable, rather than be left in uncertainty. You are, Miss Irwin, most dear to me. I love you with a strong and fervent love, which I cannot if I would conquer. Is the confession one which I may make with hopefulness as to your reply? Upon that reply depends my peace of mind; in your hands rests the happiness or unhappiness of my future. May I be so blessed as to be endowed with your love? You do not blame me, I trust, for being this distinct? Could I be otherwise? Would it elevate me in your esteem if I were? The whole story that I would tell is that I have lost my heart to you, and that I am eagerly seeking yours, but do not know if it is mine or not. One line from you will make me happy or miserable – may it make me happy!

Yours with respect,

And here, under the somewhat formal closing, the paper has been delicately torn completely across the page above the signature, leaving any reader in doubt as to who penned these heartfelt words to my grandmother. We'll never know. But Ella cared enough to keep the memory of that admirer for the rest of her life.

Rance, however, won the battle for Ella's heart. On August, 16, 1907, he wrote (although somewhat too briefly for my taste) of their upcoming marriage.

My Dear One, Your welcome letter received today and while I think maybe I will finish up were in a few days you need not count on seeing me so soon that there is no need of writing. We have some more contracts but I'm going to hire a man in my place and we will go anyway. I am glad to hear Bessie will be able to stand up with us. I see she is the lead in the Journal contest. Do you know who she gave the Alaskan trip to?...

Yours with love and kisses until we meet,

Your own, Rance

* * * * *

George LoRance Ladd and Ella Mae Irwin were married on September 11, 1907. In an old antique trunk that may have been one which made its way across the Oregon Trail, I have my Granny Ladd's wedding dress.

Both the skirt and underskirt are of fine white cotton with a waistline of not more than twenty-one inches. From about knee length to the bottom of the skirt are two bands of lace separated by wider bands of fabric, each detailed by narrow rows of tucks. The bodice is a very delicate, sheer fabric. It has a high neckline and long-sleeves, with an inset of net in a floral design. In the same storage bag is another beautiful bodice, ecru in color, with netting and lace, also very delicate in appearance. Although it also has a high collar, there is a V-shaped lace inset which is bordered by a row of darker ecru, almost golden colored disks, created from fine embroidery floss, that extend to the bottom of the blouse. These same golden disks, looking akin to buttons, but decorative only, are repeated the length of the sleeves. Ella must have been a beautiful bride.

Just where they lived for the first month of their wedding, I don't know, but in October, Ella was at her parents' in Carson, and Rance was working in Durkee, eighty miles or so south and west of Carson. Rance writes on October ninth:

My Dear Wife, Today is the 4th week since our wedding and since I can't be with you, I will write you a few lines to let you know I'm thinking of you and send you my love, sweetheart mine.

The folks were glad to see me and Mrs. S. is trying her best to founder me on fried chicken and Boston baked beans, also cream and a few things like that.

I stayed Sunday night in Halfway and played some solo at Taylors. Got here at 12 o'clock and hardly went out for a walk. I don't know quite how long I will stay here. Charlie and I have considerable work to do.

It seems that Rance was always off to another job, another contract, before they settled in Cornucopia where he went to work at the Last Chance Mine.

18

Eventually, he became the superintendent of the mine. It was into this setting that my mother, Catherine Vera Ladd, later called Catherine Veronica Ladd, was born on December 23, 1909. With snow often as high as sixteen feet, according to the *Pine Valley Echoes,* the family would spend the winters down in Pine Valley, but Mother always listed her birthplace as Cornucopia, so I'm presuming Ella birthed her first child high up on the mountain.

Rance must have been making a fair wage at the time as the *Pine Valley Echoes* writes that "he drove a new Oakland car when cars were first sold here in about 1918." Mother remembers starting school in San Diego and their spending time in California during the years at the end of World War I.

My brother asked, as he interviewed Mother many years later, "What was your dad doing there?" "Oh, he was entertaining the troops," she said. "He always had plenty of friends." Rance must have been a natural raconteur. Back in Cornucopia he had played music in bars and, undoubtedly, he had a repertoire which the boys in the service of their country would enjoy.

Stories in the *Pine Valley Echoes* report that a fire in 1920 destroyed all the buildings at the Last Chance Mine. Another story tells of a change in ownership. Did Rance lose his job?

For whatever the reason, Rance and Ella Ladd, with their daughter Catherine, moved to Kellogg, Idaho, in 1923, where they settled on South Division Street, near the community of Wardner. After Ella's father's death in Carson, her mother, Mary Catherine Irwin, came to live with them in Kellogg.

In 1924, twin boys, James and John, called Jimmy and Jack, were born to my grandmother and grandfather, and, in 1927, a second daughter, Lois,

19

arrived. Sadly, in 1931, Jimmy was hit by an automobile and killed while sledding down the street near their home. He is buried in the small cemetery on a hill overlooking the town.

Always on the lookout for a better strike, in 1937, Rance and two other men obtained a lease on a property, the Clara Morris Vein, in Gibbonsville, another Idaho gold mining town almost two hundred and fifty miles south of Kellogg, thirteen miles from the Montana border.

There, in June of the same year, George LoRance Ladd, away from his home and family, became ill and died. Ella had no money to bring his body back to Kellogg for a burial in the Kellogg cemetery near his son, Jimmy. Ella's brother, Johnnie (J.F.) Irwin, paid the city of Salmon, the closest town to Gibbonsville, $26.50 for a gravesite, and he paid William C. Doebler, of the William C. Doebler Mortuary in Salmon, who provided everything necessary, including a suit, to inter Rance's body in the Salmon cemetery, the sum of $250.00. There was also a five dollar charge for one spray of flowers. No provision for a gravestone was included in the invoice.

In 2008, while visiting in Idaho, I went to Salmon to search for my grandfather's gravesite. The green-grassed cemetery lies on a hillside overlooking the small community and the Salmon River, the River of No Return, and the birthplace of Sacajawea. There is still no marker, but I found the location of George LoRance Ladd's grave from records in the cemetery office. I walked uphill until I found the approximate site, then searched among the rows until I found the names of the two people, as the record indicated, buried on either side of him. As I stood gazing across the valley, it saddened me to think that he should have died so alone and away from his family. It grieved me to think of my grandmother, Ella, not being at his bedside to say goodbye.

Ella continued to live in Kellogg, in a small three-bedroom home at 716 South Division Street, for the rest of her life. She cleaned houses, took in ironing, and cared for the children of several doctors' families in Kellogg. She attended St. Rita's Catholic Church, walking to Mass each Sunday. Her oldest daughter, Catherine, had moved to the Philippine Islands before Rance's death. Her surviving son, Jack, was what we might now recognize as being minimally disabled, having a medical condition related to epilepsy. He worked at menial jobs, was very well liked in the community, never married, and lived with his mother until her death. After her high school graduation, Ella's younger daughter, Lois, left for nursing school in Spokane, Washington, and was almost immediately drawn to become a nun in the Sisters of Providence order. Taking the name of Sister Marie Emmeline, Lois became a nurse, earned a master's degree, and later co-founded the first Birthing Center in the Spokane area.

The World War II years must have been very difficult for my Granny Ladd as Catherine and Paul and their three children had been trapped in the Philippine Islands at the start of the war. She must have prayed fervently for their safe return to the States. No doubt it was a bittersweet day in her life when she received the following telegram from Washington, DC:

SKA 54. 62 GOVT=WUX WASHINGTON DC FEB 23 547P 1945:

=MRS. ELLA M LADD= 716 SOUTH DIVISION ST KELLOGG IDAHO

=AM PLEASED TO INFORM YOU THAT INFORMATION RECEIVED INDICATES THE RESCUE BY OUR FORCES OF YOUR DAUGHTER CATHERINE

L CRAWFORD PHYSICAL CONDITION POOR AND PAULINE S CRAWFORD DONALD L CRAWFORD PHYSICAL CONDITION FAIR FORMERLY INTERNED AT SANTO TOMAS STOP YOU MAY SEND FREE THROUGH AMERICAN PRISONER OF WAR INFORMATION BUREAU THIS OFFICE ONE ONLY TWENTY FIVE WORD MESSAGE STOP=
LE RCH PROVOST MARSHAL GENERAL

There was, however, no mention of her youngest granddaughter, my sister Sharon, or Paul, my father, in the telegram. Granny must have thought they had died during the war. It was not until later that she learned we had all survived. Granny Ladd did not come to California to meet us when our ship arrived in San Francisco. Over a week later we were all reunited in Kellogg.

When our family set up housekeeping in Kellogg for a short time following our return from the war, my great-grandmother, Mary Catherine Irwin, now 86 years old, was still living with Granny Ladd. I recall her memory was fading, yet there were some things of which she was quite aware. One evening Ella was talking about her own siblings and had asked her mother about one or the other of them. Great-grandma Irwin retorted, "Good Lord, Ella, don't you know Johnnie?"

On the Fourth of July of that same year, Great-grandma died. Following her funeral Mass at St. Rita's, her body was interred in the family plot in the Pine Valley Cemetery in Halfway, Oregon, where she had lived most of her life and raised her family.

After my father, Paul, died in 1964, Mother, with my two younger sisters, moved back to Kellogg from California, where they had been living for several years. Mother eventually bought a small house on Silver Street, less than a block away from Granny Ladd's home. I'm sure it gave Ella comfort to have her older daughter and youngest granddaughters living so close by.

On May 5, 1973, Ella Mae Ladd succumbed to lung cancer. She was puzzled; she had never smoked a day in her life, she said. (At the time, we knew nothing about second-hand smoke, but both her husband and her son, Jack, were heavy smokers.)

Like her mother, Granny Ladd's funeral Mass was held at St. Rita's in Kellogg, and following the funeral, her body was buried near her mother's grave in Halfway, Oregon, in the same small Pine Valley Cemetery that looks up toward the Granite Mountains where she had grown up.

Ten days after Granny's death, my own mother had a stroke. Although it was not permanently debilitating, Mother wasn't up to cleaning out Granny's house so it could be either rented or sold. I was teaching at the time, but as soon as school was out in June, I flew up to Kellogg to see how I could help.

I don't think Granny ever threw anything away and she had lived in the same house for almost fifty years. There were papers and records dating back to those earliest days. We found old letters, bits of money in dresser drawers, and Christmas gifts of personal items (some still in their tissue wrapping paper) that had never been worn. We couldn't keep everything.

One of the saddest things I've ever had to do in my life was to dispose of that which we could not keep or give away. I borrowed a pickup truck from a local auto dealer, which, in a small town like Kellogg where everyone knew my grandmother, was not difficult to do. Then, in three trips, I loaded boxes, magazines, old letters, you-name-it, all evidence of eighty-seven years of living, into the bed of that pickup, drove a few miles out of town, and tossed the loads on the city dump. *How sad,* I thought, *to come to the end of your life and have your memories end up on a city dump.* It was heart-wrenching. I've never really gotten over it.

I wish I had a grander array of personal memories of my Granny Ladd. Mostly, I see her standing in her large kitchen, washing and ironing other families' clothes. She was forever serious; I don't remember her ever being light-hearted, smiling, or telling a joke. It's likely she was often worried about what might happen to her son, Jack, after she was gone. (Following her death he lived independently, but looked to my mother, until her death, to assist him in handling his affairs. When Mother died, my youngest sister, Terry, who lived nearby, took on the responsibility.)

Among some of Ella's memorabilia I found while cleaning out her house, was a poem, copied on a half-sheet of blue-lined notepaper in her own distinctive handwriting.

"Life's Clock"
> *The clock is wound but once,*
> *and no man has the power,*
> *to tell just where the hands will stop,*
> *at late or early hour—*
> *to lose one's wealth is sad indeed,*
> *to lose one's health is more:*
> *to lose one's soul is such a loss*
> *as no man can restore:*
> *The present only is our own—*
> *Live, love, toil with a will—*
> *Place no faith in tomorrow—*
> *The clock may then be still—*

This Ella seemed far removed from the young girl who wrote to her loving Rance in 1905:

> *"There is going to be a dance at Hathaway's Friday night. It will be a Hard Times dance and no supper.*

Johnnie Ludiker is going to play the violin and my brother Johnnie is going to play the organ. I think I will go with him. I wish you could be here to go with me. I will miss several good dances with you..."

Oh, that we could dance again, as in our youth.

Chapter 3 ...by a Hard Rock Miner

Paul Rexford Crawford

Between 1903 and 1936

My father always described himself as being just a 'hard rock miner.' What he didn't add was that he had worked at his trade in North and South America, Asia and the Philippine Islands. He might also have described himself as somewhat of an adventurer.

I don't have any souvenirs Daddy may have owned as a child, and I don't have any pictures of him as he was growing up. But I do have a treasure trove of letters, notebooks, old passports and other souvenirs from his early adult years that have given flesh and bones and substance to my memories of my father as I knew him.

Paul Rexford Crawford, born in 1903 in Germfask, Michigan, was the fourth child of Hugh and Matilda Crawford, of whom I've written about earlier. And, as I've also mentioned, theirs was not a happy household. My mother once told me Daddy hardly ever smiled when they first met. In my mind, he was always serious, always thinking.

My father was thirteen or fourteen years old in 1917, when Matilda moved with her children to Mullan, Idaho, where Dad went to high school for three years before he enlisted in the army.

Among the letters, notebooks and other remembrances of my father's life, which Mother kept in a cedar chest at the foot of her bed, was an employment application form Dad had completed in 1946, when he applied to work at the American Smelting and Refining Company, in their Mexican Mining Department. The record of employment begins with the year 1920, when he wrote that he was in the US Army from December 1920 to December 1923. Mother told me that he lied about his age in order to be eligible to enlist. Where he was stationed I have no idea, and my efforts to uncover this information hit a brick wall, when, in response to a letter which I had written, the National Personnel Records Center informed me a fire in 1973, "had destroyed the major portion of records of Army personnel for the period 1912 through 1959." As far as I know he was never in combat. My brother thinks Dad served some time in Hawaii as he recalls Dad telling him that the nights were so bright *"I could read a newspaper by the light of the moon."* The only remark Dad ever made to me in reference to his being in the service was the comment in a letter to me, when I had been 'campused' in college for some infraction of the rules, that I'd be lucky if I spent half as much time 'campused' as he had spent in the brig when he was in the army.

Once discharged, Paul returned home to Mullan, and began working in the lead and silver mines in the area. For the next six years, he worked in various mines in the Coeur d'Alene Mining District. It was here that he learned his trade as a hard rock miner. This meant spending eight hours underground with only artificial light to work by. Probably as one of the youngest men, and low man on the shift in his early years, his job would have been to use a pick to break up rock along the vein of ore, then shovel the ore into a tram where it would be hauled to the surface and trucked to a mill for refining. Although the damage would not show up for many years, breathing the stale underground air began, in a most insidious way, to take its toll on Paul's lungs.

Now in his early twenties, it wasn't 'all work and no play' for Paul. Although not a tall man, at five-feet ten-inches, he was lean and good-looking. He had dark brown hair with a prominent widow's peak, and heavy brows over deep brown eyes. He was always a serious man, as Mother would describe later, and intelligent. He loved to read.

He must have been attracted to the sweet, shy, pretty girl named Catherine Ladd who had been the valedictorian of her high school class two years before. Mother recalled her first date with Paul:

I was on a picnic with a great big crowd up at Pottsville, [near Mullan] a place where we all used to go. When it was time to go home Paul was pairing everyone up and I was the only one left. I didn't have a date so he took me home. We went together until he went to Russia.

Why did my dad decide to take a job in Russia? My cousin Mary Ann Denning, whose father, Maurice, my father's younger brother, also worked in the mines, told me the following story.

The Great Depression, begun in 1929, had a major impact on employment in the Idaho panhandle. The opportunity to work was at a premium. The assigning of day crews in the Silver Valley mining area was coordinated by a man nicknamed 'King Cole,' who was employed by the mine owners. Workers were hired at his whim. He required that each man who wanted to work show up every day to be assigned—or not—as he saw fit. Mary Ann says that for some reason Paul didn't show up at one of these daily roll calls and was blackballed by King Cole. Without King Cole's blessing, there was no job to be found in the Silver Valley. And, to compound matters, Catherine, who had stayed home a year after her high school graduation, and whom he had been dating, was getting ready to leave Idaho to attend college in San Diego, California.

During these early years working for various mining companies, Paul had caught the eye of a contractor named A. J. May, who was impressed with Paul's work and took him under his wing. A. J. May's business was headquartered in Salt Lake City, Utah, and he was well enough known to have been in communication with the Amtorg Trading Corporation, a Russian company, established in New York in 1924 by Armand Hammer, to increase the import-export business between the United States and the Soviet Union. During this period Joseph Stalin began his first Five Year Plan, and needed men to teach the Russians better ways of mining.

On September 6, 1930, a Mr. S. M. Soupcoff from Amtorg telegraphed Mr. May, and a series of Western Union telegrams went back and forth between the Amtorg New York office, Mr. May in Salt Lake City, Utah, and Paul Crawford in Mullan, Idaho.

WESTERN UNION

RECEIVED AT 278 MAIN ST., CLIFT BLDG. SALT LAKE CITY, UTAH
1930 SEP 6 AM 10:48

JACK MAY=
CARE UNIVERSITY CLUB SALTLAKECITY UTAH=

WANT EXCELLENT FOREMAN THOROUGHLY ACQUAINTED WITH SHAFT SINKING OPERATION STOP SALARY FOUR HUNDRED PER MONTH

LOCATION OF WORK RUSSIA STOP CONTRACT TWO YEARS CAN YOU LET US HAVE JACK AJO OR SOMEONE EQUALLY AS GOOD WIRE ANSWER KARMASHOV AMTORG TRADING CORPORATION 261 FIFTH AVENUE NEWYORK=

S M SOUPCOFF.

Upon receiving the telegram, Mr. May responded to Soupcoff and Karmashov recommending Paul Crawford, and then he immediately sent a telegram to my father in Mullan.

WESTERN UNION

RECEIVED AT 10:10 AM

SALT LAKE CITY UTAH (SENT AT 9:45 A.M.)

SEPT 8, 1930

PAUL CRAWFORD

BOX 574

MULLAN IDAHO

(Handwritten in pencil)

JOB FOUR HUNDRED MONTH RUSSIA

TAKE IT WIRE AT ONCE.

A.J. MAY.

A. J. May's recommendation was all that was needed for Paul to find a new employer. Both Soupcoff and Karmashov sent their acceptances.

WESTERN UNION

JACK MAY=

CARE UNIVERSITY CLUB SALTLAKECITY UTAH= 1930 – SEP 8 AM 7 18

WILL TAKE PAUL CRAWFORD STOP HAVE HIM GET IN TOUCH WITH KARMASHOV AND YOU WIRE KARMASHOV DIRECT RECOMMENDING HIM FOR THE JOB KINDEST REGARDS
SOUPCOFF

WESTERN UNION

JACK MAY=
UNIVERSITY CLUB SALTLAKECITY UTAH=

RETEL 7 YOUR RECOMMENDATION SATISFACTORY MAILING LETTER=
KARMASHOV

Some of my father's leadership characteristics begin to show up in this exchange of telegrams. Paul wanted more information about what he was getting himself into. Perhaps he sent Mr. May a telegram inquiring about the conditions he would be encountering. He received this reply:

(*Written in pencil*)
RECEIVED AT 8:40 AM – 9/11
SALT LAKE CITY UTAH SEPT. 10 – 1930

PAUL R. CRAWFORD
MULLAN, IDA

CLIMATE SAME MONTANA JOB SHAFT FOREMAN THEY PAY ALL EXPENSES SALT LAKE TO EUROPE RAILROAD FARE EUROPE ONLY SALARY STARTS DAY YOU SAIL HALF-PAID AMERICAN HALF RUSSIAN MONEY STOP
YOU NEED ABOUT THREE HUNDRED FOR CLOTHING AND INITIAL EXPENSES PHONE OR WIRE ME TOMORROW
    MUST RUSH

A. J. MAY

How lucky I feel that this next letter from Mr. May to Mr. Karmoshov did not get lost in the eighty years since it was written:

Amtorg Trading Corporation
261 Fifth Avenue
New York City, N.Y.
Gentlemen: Attention: Mr. Karmoshov
Re: TBZ 304-908

In reply to your letter of Sept. 8, I have had Mr. Paul R. Crawford, the man preferred by Mr. Soupcoff, for your shaft job in Russia, write you in detail today.

I can recommend Mr. Crawford as being thoroughly capable and having a good knowledge of American shaft sinking methods as well as a thorough knowledge of all underground workings.

I am satisfied that he will prove an excellent foreman. We consider him one of the best foremen that we have ever had.

By September 13, 1930, Paul had left Idaho and gone to stay at the University Club in Salt Lake City, where A.J. May was living (or where he was a member). From there Paul sent a formal letter, with all the pertinent information that Amtorg might need to know before hiring him. He claimed to have been born in 1900. (Did he add a few years onto his birth date to seem more mature since he had just reached his twenty-seventh birthday?) He also claimed to have graduated from high school. He detailed his experience, listed references and enclosed a photograph. "Four hundred dollars ($400) per month is the minimum salary acceptable," he wrote.

On September 18, Karmashov wires back:

ORDER PASSPORT GIVE OUR MAILING ADDRESS WEEK LATER LEAVE FOR NEW YORK PREPARED TO SAIL.

On the back of this telegram, in Paul's handwriting, is written:

70% US Currency

30% Rubles

1st class RR fair Europe

Taking nothing for granted, the next day Paul sends another telegram to Karmashov stating his requirements:

(Typed – not Western Union style)

> Salt Lake City, Utah
> September 19, 1930

V. Karmashov, Technical Bureau,
Amtorg Trading Corporation
261 Fifth Avenue, New York.

SALARY TERMS NOT ACCEPTABLE REQUIRE SEVENTY PERCENT GOLD AND THIRTY RUBLES ALSO FIRST CLASS EUROPEAN RAILROAD ACCOMMODATIONS STOP WILL SIGN CONTRACT THESE TERMS STOP IF ACCEPTABLE SEND TWO HUNDRED FIFTY DOLLARS TRAVELLING EXPENSES AND WILL LEAVE IMMEDIATELY STOP ON RECEIPT OF WIRE REPLY WILL APPLY FOR PASSPORT.

> P. R. Crawford

Salt Lake Address, University Club

On September twentieth the deal was sealed. From V. Karmashov at Amtorg came the acceptance of Paul's conditions:

TERMS ACCEPTABLE TELEGRAPH EXPENSE TO COPPER NATIONAL BANK

> P. R. CRAWFORD C/O A.J. MAY

Ten days later, less than a month from receiving the first offer, Paul prepared to leave for Russia. On the back of the letter from Karmashov he wrote to his mother, Matilda, who was still living in Mullan. He wrote he had been making arrangements for her to be able to withdraw money from his bank account should she have a need. He also cautioned her to save all records in the event something might go awry.

130 ½ Regent Ste.
Oct. 1 - 30

Mother:

Am leaving Salt Lake tonite at 7:00—have not heard from you or got that card from the bank so if you have sent it all ready it will probably be sent back and you can send it to the bank yourself just address it "The National Copper Bank"—Am sending you a sample of the kind of slip you will have to fill out in case you want to draw. Would like for you to save these notes in case of trouble—also am going to send the bank a copy of my contract and they will forward it to you and be sure to save that also.

Well Mother will write as I go along so good bye for now.

Paul

Next, he wrote, in his usual terse, matter-of-fact fashion, a letter to Catherine who was back in Kellogg after attending college in San Diego for only one year. While they had been dating, they were not yet formally engaged to be married.

New York City, October 10, 1930

Dear Catherine: This is to say hello also good bye for I leave this P.M. at 8 o'clock on the Majestic for Southampton England and another boat from there to Leningrad and then train, boats, and horses from there. Will drop a line as I go along.

Paul

It was exciting for me to find Daddy's name on the *Majestic*'s passenger list arriving in Southampton on October 17, 1930. At the time, the RMS *Majestic,* formerly the SS *Bismarck,* purchased by the White Star Line, was the largest steamer in the world. It held over two thousand passengers. Did he travel first class, second class, or third class? Dad had told my brother that he had played bridge with Pearl S. Buck on one of his ocean crossings, so I checked to see if her name was on the *Majestic's* passengers' manifest. There it was: Pearl Sydenstricker Buck. Could it be the same? I referred to Pearl S. Buck's biography to confirm that Sydenstricker was her middle name. It was. In 1930, she had not yet published her most well-known novel, *The Good Earth,* winner of a Pulitzer Prize in 1932. Eight years later, in 1938, she was the first American to win a Nobel Prize for Literature. I would love to have been a little birdie perched on the back of a chair at that bridge table. I wonder what they talked about. Were they partners or opponents at those bridge games on the *Majestic?*

Through their letters to one another, Paul and Catherine kept in touch. None of Mom's letters to Dad have survived, but she kept many of those he wrote to her. In one dated February 15, 1931, he wrote from Ridder Zinc - Ridder, Semipalatinsk – Okrug, U.S.S.R., describing exactly where he was working:

> *...I do not know of any other place that I could have gone and been any further away from civilization. This place is just about on the other side of the globe from you – Long. 84° E and Lat. 50°-20"N – to be exact....This place is located in the province of Kakastan in Siberia and is known as Deep Asia and*

only about twelve hundred miles from Peking China by the old Camel Caravan Trail...

And, in continuing to answer some questions she had posed, he wrote:

> *Yes, very cold. In some parts of Russia there is but little difference in dress but mostly they dress to suit the climate. This is a Mining district and Ridder is the best in Russia...I have fairly comfortable quarters but the food?*

As well as reporting the lack of palatable food and inability of any maid (he hired three and was looking for another at the time) to cook his food, Dad described the place as one *"where the Tzar sent all of the worst criminals into exile and now the Soviet is sending their prisoners here—then there is quite a few Cossacks here and between the lot we have one grand and glorious time. I can get by fairly well with the men but the more I am around the she-male type the less that I think of them in general."*

Paul also included personal notes in these letters to Catherine. He told her he was sorry to hear that she had left college in San Diego and had gone back to her home in Kellogg. He said that if he'd known that, he might have asked her to go to Russia with him. He missed her, I could tell.

One of the treasures that Paul brought home to Catherine was an icon in a dark wooden shadow box holding a picture of Christ the Pantocrator. The face of Jesus, holding up his right hand, three fingers curved inward in a blessing gesture, is surrounded by a layer of gold which has never lost its luster. A red votive candle holder was attached to the bottom of the frame. Although he was not a practicing Catholic, Paul knew how much this gift would mean to Catherine. Throughout most of her life, this icon hung on a wall of Mother's bedroom.

When her health seriously declined, she gave it to me, and it hung in our living room for many years. When I moved to a condo in San Clemente I gave it to my sister, Sharon, where it now hangs in their living room.

Whatever reasons Paul had for leaving his job I don't know, but in June or early July, 1931, he left the U.S.S.R. He had been away from home less than a year. From Ridder, where he was working, he traveled east to Japan, then back to the United States across the Pacific Ocean on the Japanese liner, *Tatsuta Maru*, departing from Yokohama, Japan, on July 16, and arriving in Los Angeles, California on August 1, 1931, well before the start of World War II. A souvenir passenger list from the *Tatsuta Maru* includes the names of my dad and his good friend, Chester Dorsey, who was also a miner, and who had also been employed by Amtorg on the same project.

Paul was not long out of work. The next letter written to Catherine came from Winton, Wyoming, postmarked October 24, 1931. Finding this letter was like coming across a little missing piece of a jigsaw puzzle for me. My brother, in talking to me about Dad's past, had told me that Dad had also worked in a coal mine. When I think of coal mines, I think first of Pennsylvania, and then of West Virginia or Kentucky. There's no period in the time frame of Dad's life I could imagine his living in those parts of the country. As I discovered, Winton, located in

Sweetwater County, and now a ghost town with no buildings left standing, had once been a coal-mining community.

This letter speaks of Paul's longing to have Catherine with him as his wife. I'm surmising this isn't the first proposal Mother received from him, but I note a sense of urgency in his tone as he goes on to say that he has another job in California coming up in the spring and that they should *"have enough in the sock to last for a while any way."* He ends with the plea, *"so hurry Honey and answer this or take an airplane down and answer it in person would be better still. Till Niagra Falls. Always, Paul"*

Catherine didn't come down to Winton, Wyoming. Nor did she go to Boulder City, Nevada in December of that year, 1931, where Paul was now working at the construction site of the Boulder Dam (now renamed Hoover Dam). In one of her letters, Mom had evidently asked a question her father had asked her to ask Paul about working conditions at the dam site. Rance was wondering if there might also be a job for him. He always seemed to be looking for a better opportunity to hit pay dirt. Paul writes:

Your dad wanted to know if it was under government supervision—it is supposed to be but there is a suit on now in the courts to determine if this is a reservation or State of Nevada against Six Co. Inc. & Federal Government.

The wage scale here is $.50 per hour for common labor—$5.00 per shift for chuck tenders and $5.60 per day for miners - $8.00 per day for shift bosses and by the way, I have the promise of the next opening as shift boss. Don't know of any other details that your dad would like to know ...except it might be a good idea when registering at the employment office in Las Vegas

38

to register as both mine and chuck tender, one stands
a better chance of going to work sooner.

Time passed slowly for Paul.

*Saturday night and no place to go and have all my
crossword puzzles worked so thot* [sic] *I would drop
you a few lines..."*

He tells her he hasn't heard from her and asks if she
has found a boyfriend that is keeping her busy. He's
frustrated, for sure.

*I get so d— disgusted with this place some times
that it is hard to stay and wish that they would lay me
off. They finished one of the tunnels on the Arizona
side today and all but three of the miners got layed
off—we will finish the one that I am in next week some
time and am hoping that they will lay me off too...I sure
wish that we could drop up home tonite and have some
of Mother's beer and visit the old parking place and
everything...*

Although I don't have any of my mother's letters to
Paul, I know she agreed to become engaged, as he wrote
in a reply:

*February 28 – '32... Dear Catherine, Received both of
your letters several days ago and have been waiting
for a letter with a check in it so that I could send you
the rest to pay on that ring but it has not arrived yet so
if it does not come by tomorrow I will send this letter on
without it and the money later... A Lonesome Boy, Paul*

In pencil, added later, he wrote,

*Las Vegas P.S. Got check OK but had to leave it
here at bank for collection so it will be another ten days
before I have the cash.*

No more letters. Whatever transpired in the next
seven months is between Paul and Catherine, but my
parents were married at the St. Joan of Arc Catholic
Church in Las Vegas, Nevada, on September 2, 1932. I

have no wedding pictures, nor any letters which revealed details about their wedding. I do have the Las Vegas Bureau of Records letter which confirmed the date and location of their marriage.

Paul was still employed at the Boulder Dam at the time. However, Mother never spoke about living in Nevada, so I'm conjecturing that shortly after their marriage they moved to California.

They were living in Beaumont, California when I was born in 1933. Daddy was working on the California aqueduct being constructed at the time. Whether the aqueduct job was finished, or Dad got itchy feet, or he didn't like the way the operation was going, I don't know, but he left the aqueduct project and found work, as noted on another resume I've found among Mother's papers, as a rock drill demonstrator for the Worthington Machinery Company in Los Angeles, a general foreman at the Tujunga Rock Quarry and, as a miner in a copper mine in Miami, Arizona. He was working in Arizona when he got the offer to go to work in a gold mine on the island of Luzon in the Philippine Islands.

In September, 1936, Paul sailed from San Francisco to Manila on the SS *Hoover*. Mother and I returned to her home in Kellogg, where we waited until my father sent for us.

Chapter 4 ...by a Miner's Wife

Catherine Vera Ladd

Between 1909 and 1936

My first inclination was to title this chapter about my mother, 'by a blue-eyed Minerva,' taking the inspiration from the entry next to her name in the 1928 *Wildcat,* the yearbook of Kellogg High School, the year she, Catherine Vera Ladd, graduated as valedictorian of her class. Her photo shows her to be a quiet, smiling, dignified young woman. In the adjacent column, beside her name is a listing of the activities in which she was involved, and the phrase *'Minerva, the goddess of wisdom, personified.'* I wonder, was *Vera,* the middle name given her by her parents, a derivative of *Minerva*? What was my grandmother, Ella Ladd, thinking about in those dark December days just before her first child was born? And when did Mother make the change from Vera to Veronica, the middle name she used as long as I can remember?

In December of 1909, in Cornucopia, Oregon, which I described earlier in Chapter Two, when writing about my maternal grandparents, the snow level was just over five feet, a moderate snowfall for the eight thousand foot elevation. Two days before Christmas, on December 23rd, my mother, Catherine Vera, was born to Rance and Ella Ladd.

Whether Ella stayed up on the mountain after the baby arrived, or went down to the valley to stay for a time with her parents, I don't know, but Cornucopia was, for most of the next fourteen years, Rance, Ella, and Catherine's home until the family moved to Kellogg, Idaho, in 1923. I have a photograph of a proud Rance, pipe in his mouth, standing next to Ella atop one of the Granite Mountain peaks near the Last Chance Mine where he was the superintendent. Rance is holding Catherine, who looks to be about three, in his arms. But, as with my father, there are no photos of the house in which my mother lived, the school which she attended, no report cards, no dolls, no scraps of cloth, or remnants of a dress her mother might have sewn. Mother's main memory of Cornucopia, as she once told me, seems to have been discovering a skunk in the outhouse.

There were few children Catherine's age in Cornucopia, but Rance had a sister, Edith, who was, at the time, living in the Pine Valley, as the area which included Halfway and Cornucopia was called. Edith and her husband, Henry Mentle, were parents of an only daughter, Evangeline (named after Rance's mother), who was about the same age as Catherine. The two cousins remained friends for the rest of their lives. Another of Rance's sisters, Osa, had moved to San Diego, California. Mother remembered that she and her family also moved to San Diego for a short time in 1918, where she started school when she was eight years old.

However, my grandfather Rance couldn't seem to settle down in one place. He would return to Cornucopia with his family at least once more after 1918, and five years later, in 1923, when Catherine was fourteen, he moved his family to Kellogg, Idaho, where there were a number of working lead, zinc and silver mines where he believed he could find a job.

The story goes that Kellogg, located in the mountains of the panhandle of northern Idaho, was founded in 1885 by a prospector named Noah Kellogg and the jackass who was carrying Noah's grub and supplies. While pawing the ground in the vicinity of Noah's camp, the jackass uncovered traces of silver ore, which eventually led to the development of the mining industry in the area. The Bunker Hill and Sullivan Mine, an outgrowth of that discovery of ore, was, while it was operating, one of the richest in the country. For decades the mountain above Kellogg was called Jackass Mountain. Proud of its moniker, for years there was a billboard on US Highway 90, as you approached Kellogg, which pictured a smiling jackass with its hind quarters kicked up behind him. It read, "You are now near Kellogg, the town which was discovered by a jackass and is inhabited by its descendants." It was not until the 1970s that the mountain was renamed Silver Mountain to attract skiers to the resort which had been built there.

In her book, *The Good Times Are All Gone Now,* Julie Whitesel Weston wrote of Kellogg as a "one-horse town." (p.34) She wrote that everyone seemed to get along; there was little clannishness. "The Bunker Hill was the horse that pulled the community's wagon," she said. Nearly everyone either worked in the mine or in some related job that supported the men and families who were employed there. Whether or not my grandfather worked at the Bunker or one of the other mines in the area, and there were quite a number of them, I don't know, but not more than a mile and half down the hill from the site on the mountain where Noah Kellogg's burro uncovered the silver ore, Rance settled his family. They lived in several houses along South Division Street, which descends, in the area where they lived, like a wedge with sloping mountains rising behind the houses on each side of the street. A modest three bedroom clapboard house, at 716 South Division Street, was the home in which Ella would live for the remainder of her life. Catherine remembers starting the eighth grade after they moved to Kellogg. Rance, ever the prospector, travelled between Idaho and Oregon. He went to wherever he believed the treasure under the earth could make him a living.

In 1924, the year her twin brothers, Jimmy and Jack, were born, Catherine enrolled as a student at Kellogg High School, a two-storied brick building situated only a long block from where her family lived. (This was the same building, which later became Kellogg Junior High School when the new high school was built, and where I attended the eighth grade for the 1945-1946 school year.)

As well as excelling academically, Catherine had a beautiful voice and was a member of a Girls' Sextet and Chorus. Her senior yearbook also lists a 'Ninety Club' and G.E.M. Club. Her achievements were not lost on the yearbook editor who identified her, as I've already noted, *"Minerva, the goddess of wisdom, personified."*

"Catherine Ladd," the *Kellogg Evening News* clipping noted early in May, 1928, "has been appointed valedictorian of the graduating class of 1928, having a scholastic standing of 94.53 % for the four years." (My mom might be aghast that I'd put her achievement out there for all the world to see, but during her lifetime she was so modest and so willing to let others shine in the limelight, I think it is about time to give her a well-deserved moment in the sun.)

As valedictorian of the class of 1928, it was Catherine's honor to address the student body, the faculty, parents and guests who had come to the graduation ceremony. Interestingly, she chose to identify the class in military parlance as 'the 28th Company of the Kellogg Division of Schools.' She begins: "Our enlistment as students in the schools of Kellogg is now a thing of the past and my assembled classmates and I, having completed our training and maneuvers in the service, are to receive our honorable discharge and be dispersed."

As is usual in a commencement address, she challenged her fellow classmates "not to abandon ourselves to sloth and trifling. We must never stop being students, and a student whose life is one long, never-ceasing encounter with the foes of learning."

(So there's where I got my love of learning.)

I can only imagine, on that night, Catherine Ladd, must have had dreams of continuing her education in the halls of higher learning, expecting one day to graduate from a college or university.

Among the faded envelopes Mother kept is one addressed, in beautiful penmanship, to *Catherine Vera Ladd – Kellogg, Idaho.* It reads:

Pauline Crawford Crabb

May 24, 1928

Dear Catherine,

We were very proud of you tonight and so far you have a very enviable record on your school work. I enclose a little graduation gift. Put it in your sock and when you need it a little worse than you do now, dig it up and spend it and when it comes down to a pinch and you need some more if no other way presents itself, I'll oil up the old 30-30 and go out and get the bacon.

Aff—

Your "Dad"

In noting the formal address on the envelope from her father: *Catherine Vera Ladd – Kellogg, Idaho,* I'm wondering if Rance wasn't off prospecting somewhere and not able to be present at his daughter's graduation ceremony.

Catherine did not go away to college that fall. Instead, she found a job in Kellogg, and, if I know my mother well, she saved most of her salary, looking forward to enrolling in college in the near future.

Living at home, Catherine led an active social life with the group of friends she had made over the previous five years. One such get-together was a picnic up at Pottsville, a wide spot in the road along the Old Yellowstone Trail, about twelve or fifteen miles from Kellogg. This Sunday outing saw the beginning of a romance with a man six years her senior, a man named Paul Crawford who lived with his family in nearby Mullan. Paul, like Catherine's father, worked in one of the mines in the area.

Paul and Catherine 'went together' (Mother's words) until the following fall when she left for San Diego, California, to enroll in college there. Paul, finding work sparse in the Idaho panhandle, accepted a position in

Russia. However, he didn't want Catherine to forget him. On October 10, 1930, from New York City, he wrote her a brief note saying he was leaving that evening on the first leg of his journey to Russia, and telling her he would write as he went along.

I'm a bit puzzled as to whether Catherine travelled to San Diego by herself or whether one of her relatives accompanied her. She used the plural pronoun *we* when writing to her mother, recounting her four-day adventure from Spokane to San Diego on busses. "*The one we had today had a glass top,*" she wrote, "*they are all equipped with nice curtains and electric lights and little mirrors, etc.*" However, she doesn't mention her travelling companions by name.

The letters read like a travelogue as she described her journey, winding through the curvy mountain roads of Oregon, the foggy coast of northern California, having their luggage opened for an agricultural inspection, and spending nights at the Hotel Vance in Eureka, and at the Pickwick Hotel in San Francisco. She also writes of staying at the Baltimore Hotel in Los Angeles. (Built in 1896, this hotel was located at Seventh and Olive Streets, and is now the site of the Los Angeles Athletic Club's headquarters.)

Because I now live in San Clemente, California, I was thrilled to read Mother's description of my little town, as it appeared to her in September of 1929:

In San Clemente, all the houses are white stucco with little red tile roofs. It is more like a resort right on the beach or near there. All the houses and little stores and everything are just exactly alike except that they vary in size and style. It is built on little rolling hills and there are four or five long streets all laid out in blocks.

The day following her arrival at her father's sister Osa's house, where she would be living in San Diego, her aunt accompanied Catherine, to the campus of San Diego State Teachers College where she enrolled. She wrote of the experience to her mother:

I found out that they only have a four-year course so I enrolled anyway. Aunt Osa said she would help out and if my money runs out, I can always get some kind of a job. I guess it will take about $20 a month. I have about $50 left. I paid $5 for a biology book and notebook and lab equipment.

In following letters, Catherine describes in detail how her days and weekends are spent, including who has a boyfriend (she does) and who does not. She told of two carloads of family enjoying their Thanksgiving dinner in a picnic setting.

The day was lovely and we had the most fun. The place (Vacation Camp) is in a little canyon off from the main highway, parallel to it. There were lots of big oak trees and the ground underneath was so clean and smooth. We found an old door in a house there, sort of a homemade closet door, and we put that between the running boards of the two cars for our table. We had a big canvas which we spread underneath. The turkey, dressing and potatoes were nice and warm so we had a lovely dinner. We had celery, cranberry sauce (strained), sweet tomato pickles, beet pickles, and oranges and apples and hot coffee. We found the wheel of an old wagon and had lots of fun riding around on it. We pulled it up almost to the highway and then we all got on and rode down the hill.

For whatever reason, at the end of the school year, Catherine returned to Kellogg. She said she was homesick, but most probably her parents did not have enough money to pay for another year of study. She never again set foot on a college campus as a matriculated student and lived at home for the next two years.

When my brother, in a taped interview with Mother many years later, asked if there were any regrets in her life, she said, "I would like to have graduated from college." But she quickly added, "My life would probably not have been as interesting."

Paul and Catherine's fondness for each other continued via the mail. She wrote him about returning home from San Diego, and he replied that if he'd known earlier he would have asked her to come to Russia with him. Paul was anxious to come home, and by August, 1931, he was back on American soil.

The letter trail from my father to my mother next leads to Winton, Wyoming, where Paul is working. He is now twenty-eight years old and ready to get married. He writes:

> *...thought I would drop you another line just to tell you how lonesome that it is down here and to ask you how you would like to come down here to become Mrs. Crawford or I will come up there around Xmas or as soon as this job is finished. They expect to finish here in about two months but it looks like at least a three-month job to me.*

It would take Catherine almost a year before she left Kellogg to become Mrs. Paul Crawford on September 2, 1932, at St. Joan of Arc Catholic Church in Las Vegas, Nevada. Paul was still working as a safety inspector on the construction of the Boulder Dam, but before the year was out, they had moved to Randsburg, California, and not long after that to Beaumont, California, where Paul had found a job working on another major construction project: the San Jacinto tunnel of the California aqueduct.

Mother didn't leave many records of her time in southern California. When she knew she was pregnant, she found a doctor in Los Angeles. To me, Los Angeles seems a long way from Beaumont, but I don't know the particulars. Mother and Dad did have friends in Pasadena. Perhaps she spent time with them when she came to the Los Angeles area.

I was born in Los Angeles on August 21, 1933.

During the next three years, my father held several jobs in the southern California area, as I've already described when writing about his early life. All were related to his skill with dynamite, an expertise which he had accrued through the years working in mines and tunnels. In the spring or summer of 1936, he received an offer of employment in the Philippine Islands to work in a gold mine, and he quickly accepted. When he sailed for Manila that September, Mother and I returned to Kellogg, Idaho, to stay with her parents for the next three months, when my father sent for us to join him in the Philippines.

Chapter 5 ...by My Early Years

Between 1933 and 1941

The day after I was born, August 21, 1933, my mother, from her hospital bed at the California Hospital in Los Angeles, California, wrote to her mother, Ella Mae Ladd, in Kellogg, Idaho. She began, *"Dear Mother, Well, how does it feel to be a grandmother?"* She goes on to describe how they had driven in from Beaumont where they were living after she had started having labor pains early that morning. She was visiting a friend, waiting for a doctor's appointment when her water broke. *"I told him [Paul] I'd better get to the hospital. Got to the hospital about 1:30 or 20 min. to two and Pauline arrived about 2:20. They certainly rushed around."* She also admits her disappointment that I wasn't a boy. *"It was just our luck to have a girl but she sure is cute—nice and round and not a bit red. I think I did a swell job on her if I do say so myself."*

The name on my birth certificate reads: Pauline Shirley Crawford. My first name honors my father, and my middle name, Shirley, is that of one of my father's sisters, the one to whom he felt the closest. But I was never called Pauline by my parents: my name was always Mike. Dad had wanted a boy and I was named long before I was born. Only my mother's mother, Granny Ladd, ever called me Pauline. As a matter of fact, on one occasion when I was in high school, our parish priest, Father Dougherty, happened to be at a gathering where my mother was included and he asked, "Mrs. Crawford, how is Pauline?" "Pauline who?" was my mother's reply. My sister Sharon calls me 'Mikie,' so I'm assuming that is what she heard my parents calling me when I was little. Growing up, I liked being called Mike and I kept that nickname throughout my college years. It was only when I began teaching that the name Mike was awkward to explain and I acquiesced to my given name, Pauline.

Mother spent ten days in the hospital before my father came to take her back to Beaumont. She told me that my first bed was a dresser drawer. I haven't found any written notes or many photos about their time living in Beaumont, but Mother used to tell a story about a time when she was still pregnant with me and had gone into Los Angeles on the bus for a check-up with her doctor. It was March tenth, and as she was arriving in the city, a 6.4 earthquake, centered in Long Beach, struck the area, sending undulating waves as far as Los Angeles. She remembers cars rolling up and down the streets as the pavement shifted back and forth. Mother and Dad had friends in Pasadena not far from Los Angeles at the time. Instead of returning to Beaumont, she spent the night with them.

My parents lived in Beaumont until September, 1936. My father held a number of different jobs during those three years, as I've said in an earlier chapter. In the fall of 1936, he accepted a position at the Balatoc gold mine on the island of Luzon in the Philippine Islands. When my dad sailed for Manila, Mother and I lived with Granny

Ladd and Great-grandma Irwin in Kellogg, until he sent for us.

Three months later, in December, when I was just three years old, Mother and I boarded the *Tatsuta Maru*, a major passenger liner of the NYK (Nippon Yusen Kaisha) line, from the port of Los Angeles, on our way to the Philippines. The ship docked in Tokyo and from there we took a small coastal boat to Manila. Mother said that the combination of a roiling ocean and a small boat made this leg of the journey fraught with seasickness for most of the passengers. "Mike and I were the only ones who showed up to eat," she remembers.

Daddy was at the harbor in Manila Bay to meet us when Mother and I disembarked from the small ship that had brought us from Japan. They were so happy to be together again. "Mike and I were the best travelers on the ship," Mother told him. "We were practically the only ones who didn't get sick." From Manila we were driven to the Balatoc Mine where Daddy worked. Owned and operated by Marsman and Company, it was located in the province of Benguet, in the northern area of Luzon Island.

Life was good in those early years. In one of Mother's letters to her father, dated April 27, 1937, Catherine spoke of the Balatoc mine producing half a million pesos of gold every month. The "bosses" in the mine were all

Americans who had brought their families with them from the States. She describes her life as quiet and uneventful. She mentions going into Baguio to shop; she writes of a weekend at Banang, a beach where they rented a *nipa* hut for the day and enjoyed swimming in the warm water. She tells her father that I was sick most of March and was taken to the hospital in Baguio where "Dr. Reed took out her tonsils and adenoids." Other than a sore throat for a couple of days I recovered without incident. All I remember from this time is getting to enjoy a lot of ice cream.

From Balatoc my father went to work in the Benguet Mine, in the same region. It was owned by the same company. Just when he moved a third time I don't know, but in 1941, he was working at the Itogon Mine as the mine superintendent. Bill Moule, another American hired at Itogon, wrote of my father in his book, *God's Arms Around Us* (p21):

> *Paul has a pleasing personality. He can best be described as an engineer with all the attributes of a ten-day miner. He was then about thirty-eight years of age, of slim build, and had an unlimited amount of energy. He was an exacting boss, but knew what he wanted and expected it to be done as he wanted it. If you knew your stuff, you didn't have anything to worry about. But someone who didn't, or who was stubborn about adopting Itogon methods, was in for a bad time.*

Mother describes life at Itogon as rather idyllic. I have a picture of the house we lived in, built in the style of the time and the location. While it certainly wasn't a castle, it was a very comfortable home for a girl who was a miner's daughter and the woman who was a miner's wife. We had three servant girls: an *amah,* or nanny, for me (and my sister and brother when they came along), a cook, and a *lavandera* who did the laundry and the cleaning.

Mother's days were spent playing bridge with the wives of the other men in the company. She went into Baguio about once a week to order our groceries and shop for whatever other needs we didn't have available at the camp.

In one letter to her mother, Catherine wrote:

We went over to a dinner dance over at the mess (next door) last Sunday. Everyone from here and several other couples from outside camps. We had a grand turkey dinner and danced until twelve. They have a good orchestra. The Americans bought the instruments and they play free of charge.

We have invited the bunch over here Saturday night. Am going to have sandwiches, all kinds of olives, pickles, cheese, crackers, nuts, etc—sort of help yourself, very informal, and plenty to drink so they should have a good time. Rice's have a phonograph with tubes and an amplifier, etc. like a radio so we'll use that for music.

The families Mom wrote about were all around the same age and our camp abounded with young children. In a snapshot taken in September of 1941, a dozen little children are sitting on the steps of one of the houses, celebrating Butch Pearson's third birthday. I am sitting in the top row with Patsy Robinson and Joan Biason. Patsy Robinson's father, Louis Robinson, was my dad's boss. Also in the picture are my sister, Sharon, who was born shortly after my fifth birthday, and my little brother, Donald, who was not quite one year old.

Joan, just six weeks older than I, was my special friend. Her father, Perfecto Biason (although I never heard him referred to by any name but 'Doc'), was a Filipino and the camp doctor. He had met and married Daisy, a beautiful Irish nurse, while he was a medical student in the United States, and Joan was their only child. Daisy worked with Doc as the camp nurse.

Joan and I spent all of our playtime together. Sometimes we would go down to the camp bowling alley and throw pint-sized balls at the duck-pins which one of the Filipino employees would set up for us. We both took piano lessons from Miriam King, who taught several of the other children at Itogon, and we were in the same grade at Maryknoll.

When I was four, my parents had decided it was time for me to go to school. They drove me into Baguio where the missionary order of Maryknoll nuns had built a convent and operated an elementary school. The sister in charge told my parents she thought I was a little too young to attend, but agreed to let me come on a trial basis. Mother, in her interview with my brother, said, "After about a month they said Mike was doing fine, and so she stayed."

There are only a few things I recall about being at Maryknoll. I know that Sister Marcella, Sister Hyacinth and Sister Brigida were the names of my teachers. These were the nuns who started me on a journey of faith, and are now all deceased. I was not in communication with any of them after World War II.

Occasionally, my parents would board me at the convent while they took short holidays. I remember playing among the tall pines on the property, and sliding down a steep hill on the pine needles. I also remember we stopped in the middle of our playtime each day to recite the Angelus prayer when the bells rang at noon and three o'clock. Another lesson still with me was learning to hold my two hands together in a steeple position against my chest, pointing toward heaven, thumbs crossed one over the other, while I was praying. (This posture seems a little too pious in this day and age, yet it's still my first response when called to any kind of formal prayer.) On my nightstand, even today, I keep a framed photograph of myself and my friend, Joan (now Joan Helble), in our white First Communion dresses with our veils held in place by a band of white ribbon across our foreheads, accented with a small white flower on each side. She is wearing white shoes and I am wearing black patent leather Mary Janes. We look very serious. We were six years old.

One particular story my parents used to enjoy telling about me happened while I was at still a student at Maryknoll. Perhaps I like to remember it because I think it alludes to a sense of independence which seems to have been a part of my being from the time I was very young.

Every day Joan and I were driven to Maryknoll in a bus provided by the Itogon Mining Company, which took all the students whose fathers worked in the camp to their respective schools in Baguio. One afternoon, it seems, I missed the bus which had come to take me home. "So," Mother said, "Mike just called a taxi." As I recall the story, I just got into a waiting taxi at the convent entrance, and when the driver asked, "Where to?" I replied, "Take me home." "Where is home?" "To Itogon." Imagine the bill my parents had to pay for that ride?

Monday, December 8, 1941, was a scheduled holiday from school, where I was now in the third grade. This day was the Feast of the Immaculate Conception, a day for Catholics to attend Mass, but a reprieve from classes for the children. This day remains in my memory because I did not go back to school the following day, or the following weeks, or the following months. I never again saw the interior of the walls, the classrooms, or the chapel of the Maryknoll Convent. The Japanese had invaded the Philippine Islands and our lives were changed forever.

Chapter 6 ...by Life on the Run

Between December 8, 1941 and November 1, 1942

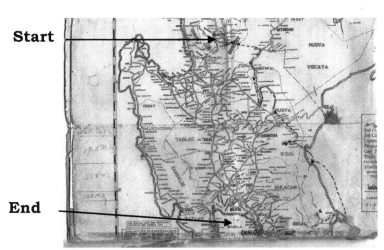

Most of the world remembers the attack on Pearl Harbor happening on December 7, 1941, but because of the International Date Line, it was already Monday, December 8, 1941, in the Philippine Islands, and the Japanese were simultaneously dropping tons of bombs on Manila Bay and the many United States military ships stationed there. World War II had begun for us. For our family and thousands of others, lives would never be the same.

Because my friend Joan and I had a reprieve from school that Monday, we were spending the day together. In her Christmas card, sixty years later to the day, Joan wrote, "You and I were playing at your house. We were suddenly taken to an abandoned tunnel not far from the camp as we watched the Jap planes fly by."

I don't remember that incident, and, although the next three and a half years were perhaps critical in some ways to my growing up, I don't consider them *the defining moments* of my life. However, I must admit, it wasn't your Dick, Jane and Spot type of early childhood for me and my two siblings.

I write about these experiences because I want to tell my children, grandchildren, and great-grandchildren how my mother and father dealt with this time of crisis in their lives. My father played a major role in our family's life as he led us safely, over a period of eleven months, from the comfort of our home at the Itogon Mine to the confines of the Santo Tomas Internment Camp in Manila.

Within days the bombing came closer and closer to home. By December 16, the local radio stations were broadcasting news of MacArthur "wanting to take down the flag at Fort Santiago because it was a target," writes Bill Moule in his book, *God's Arms Around Us.* (p.42) Shortly afterward, the radio reported Japanese troops were nearing Baguio, the closest city in our area.

At Itogon, my father and others were making plans to evacuate the mining camp.

Farther up in the mountains, north of Itogon, was the Lusod Sawmill where Louis Robinson, Dad's boss at Itogon, had already begun sending food and supplies by an aerial tramway. It was only a matter of when, not if, all the families would leave their homes. By December twenty-first, word was received from the army that all women and children were to be evacuated to Manila.

As an eight-year-old, I don't remember much of the preparation that went into abandoning our house. December 23, 1941, was my mother's thirty-second birthday. In our living room was a gaily decorated Christmas tree with a few packages under its branches. It must have been fairly traumatic for all of us to walk out of our house not being able to take any of our gifts with us. What a birthday present for Mom.

Two days later, we celebrated Christmas high up in the mountains. Mother gave me a pair of pajamas she'd been sewing for some time. "But, Mama, these pajamas are for Joan," I protested. "No, Mikie, I made them just for you." To throw me off the track, she had been telling me that she was sewing these pajamas for my friend. Joan had not come with us to Lusod, and I was hard to convince. I felt it quite unfair to be given her gift.

Once the eight or so families, along with several single men, got settled at Lusod a few of the men, including my father, went down into Baguio to buy more food. When the proprietor of the store where they usually shopped let them in the door, mobs of local Filipinos pushed their way inside as well, demanding that some of the food be sold to them. The owner advised the Americans to leave the store, drive away, and come back later through a back alley, which they did. Although the shelves were relatively empty, they stocked up on canned goods, bought all the milk he had left, and returned to the sawmill.

Only a few days after the bombing of Manila, the Japanese army had marched into Baguio. Paratroopers were landing in monumental numbers. The mayor of Baguio had announced that all Americans, as a precautionary safety measure, should bring one suitcase and go to Brent School, a prestigious private school for English-speaking students. Those who followed that advice spent the remainder of the war in that setting.

Up at Lusod, there was no consensus that the war should be waited out in the mountains. My father was certain that General MacArthur would recapture the islands in six weeks. He felt if we could get behind the enemy lines and travel to the coast we would be picked up by American ships.

Heads of families were making choices. A meeting was held. My father took charge of the meeting. Bill Moule, in *God's Arms Around Us,* set the scene this way:

Crawford was outlining the trip in the same fashion he used to outline a new project in the mine. He made a sketch on the table, all the while telling about the number of miles they should make a day, the number of horses needed, and to start with they would carry the children until they could find cargadores (native carriers).

My father thought we could reach Manila in a couple of days, and he decided we would take our chances. The last Bill Moule saw of the Itogon group who decided to try for rescue, four of the men each had a small child perched on his shoulder and were heading down the trail, either leading or pulling a pack horse. Dad was probably carrying my little brother, Donnie, who was only thirteen months old at the time. Of this trek, I remember Daddy asking me, toward evening, if I was tired, and if I would like to get up on one of the pack horses.

"I'm not tired, Daddy," I replied, "I'm just so sleepy I can't keep my eyes open." I have no idea how much ground we covered that day.

For the next eleven months, our family became fugitives from the Japanese. How long we stayed in one place, or how often we moved I couldn't say. Our group was accompanied by at least one Filipino who had worked at the mine. He, and perhaps there were others as well, would go down into the nearest villages to try to ferret news from the natives living there as to the number of Japanese in the area and the status of the war. They had to be very careful with whom they spoke for fear of disclosing information about the Americans hiding in the mountains. Not all Filipinos had remained loyal to the

Americans, but we assumed those who traveled with us had not betrayed our whereabouts. The only Filipino who has an identity for me was the *bodegero* (warehouseman). I don't know what his responsibilities were, but I'm sure he helped carry my brother and sister at times as we moved along on the steep mountainous trails. Sadly, he lost his life before the war's end.

As there were several children among the families in our camp, we were allowed to play outdoors with the stipulation that we should never ever put anything we found in our mouths. One day the temptation of bright red fruit on one of the bushes was too much, at least for me. Like Eve and the forbidden tree in the center of the garden, I picked one of the tiny red berries and plopped it into my mouth. Moments later I ran screaming back to my parents, my mouth afire. We had discovered a red pepper bush. No further punishment was necessary for disobeying the rules.

Another incident my brother related to me, as we were reminiscing on one of my visits with him, was the time my father, looking for dry firewood, picked up a big round stick protruding from under the roots of a tree only to have the stick start moving. Up from another hole on the other side of the tree came the head of a big snake.

"What kind of a snake was it?" I asked him.

"I think it was a python."

"What happened next?"

"I think I remember Dad saying they cut off its head and ate the meat."

Apocryphal tale? Who knows, but to this day, my sister Sharon, has a terrible phobia about snakes. Even coming upon a picture of one causes her to shriek.

For the next ten months, our band of Itogonites traveled in a southeasterly direction, hoping to reach a location where the Americans could rescue us. When we arrived at the coast at Dingalan Bay, which empties into the Philippine Sea, the men determined it would be faster to continue south by boat down to the mouth of the Umiray River.

Among my souvenirs from the Philippines, on the very brown fragile pages of a Bureau of Education notebook I used for school work when we were later interned in Santo Tomas, I found a composition I wrote, when I was eleven years old, about this short journey:

"Just in Time"

It was around one o'clock in the morning and the whole family was up getting ready for a short trip. It may seem strange that we were starting at that time of night, but the boatman, a bankero, would not agree to go sooner than 2:00 a.m.

The trip was to be made in a banca with sails. This type of boat is used a great deal by the Filipinos on the ocean. The day before the trip my father looked the boat over to see if he thought it were seaworthy and he concluded that the banka would be suitable for the trip across the bay.

It was now around a quarter to two and the boat was ready to push off. There were others besides our family. From Dingalan Barrio we were to sail across the bay to the mouth of the Umiray River. Immediately after starting several men were kept busy bailing the water out of the boat but instead of the water decreasing it increased more and more.

We arrived at our destination about 10:30 that morning. The women and children immediately went ashore while the men remained to unload the banca. Just as the men finished unloading and the last man stepped ashore the banca sank to the bottom of the river.

My Life Defined...
How thankful we all were that this did not happen a short time before while we were still on the ocean and in deep water.

This episode was also mentioned in *God's Arms Around Us,* probably told as old friends swapped war stories after our liberation. Perhaps this incident served to elucidate the dangers we could expect at every turn. Or perhaps the Japanese had learned about the Americans in hiding in the hills. Whatever the reason or reasons, my father decided it was time for the Crawford family to surrender.

Chapter 7 ...by a Jail Cell

Between November 1, 1942 and December 2, 1942

By November 1, 1942, we were only about 45 kilometers, or roughly 28 miles from Manila as the crow flies. At what point our family separated from the other Itogon people is not clear to me. From my father's old Socony Road Map of the island of Luzon, I can see faint, penciled dash marks where he had marked our route. As the map is slowly disintegrating and coming apart at the creases, I can barely make out the word "Daraiton," a town located almost due east of Manila. But this is not the day we would surrender.

Mother, in the neat Palmer-method penmanship of which she was most proud, kept a diary, and although the surviving notes in my little brown notebook are few, it's because of these that I've been able to piece together the sequence of the next four weeks.

According to Mom's notes, we spent November second on the trail, and on November third she wrote: "Church Tanay." Did the *bodegero* arrange with a Filipino priest to act as a go-between? Did we just stumble upon this church? Is this where the Japanese came to pick us up? We did not remain there long. On November fourth we spent the night in the Japanese military barracks at Morong, another village closer to Manila. The following day we were taken to barracks at Antipolo, still closer to Manila, and later moved to the Municipal Building in the city. During this time the Japanese officers in charge took my father away from us, interrogated him, and sent him back into the mountains to try to persuade the other Americans to surrender.

For almost a month—from November eighth to November twenty-ninth—my mother, sister, brother and I were housed in a jail cell at the Municipal Building in Antipolo. It was a cell like any other you might see on a TV program with a high window to the outside. I remember the Filipinos putting bananas through this window to supplement our food.

My sister Sharon remembers clinging behind Mom's knees. I don't remember our father being in the jail cell with us, and I'm presuming these must have been the days when he had gone back into the mountains.

On November 29, Mother wrote "Paul to P.G.H." Did the "H" stand for "hospital"? On December 1 and 2 we were moved again. Mother noted: *Nipa Cottage—c/o Military Police—Antipolo.*

From Antipolo, on December 2, 1942, the next leg of our adventure began. In Mother's words: *Dec. 2—We came to S.T.I.C.*—Santo Tomas Internment Camp. Located in Manila, we were civilian prisoners of war for the next two years and three months.

Chapter 8 ...by Santo Tomas Internment Camp

Between December, 1942 and December, 1943

Coming from a prison cell in Antipolo to the compound of buildings that comprised Santo Tomas Internment Camp in Manila, with two- to three-thousand Americans and other English-speaking people, my parents must have breathed a huge sigh of relief that the Crawford family of five was now ensconced in a safer environment. If our efforts to escape the Japanese had been less than successful, at least we were now in a situation where our presence could be accounted for.

Our new home away from home, if you could call it that, was on the grounds of the University of Santo Tomas, which was owned and administered by the Dominican order of priests. Founded in 1611, the university had occupied its present site on sixty-five acres in north Manila since 1911. Its academic programs were recognized world-wide as being equal to other pontifical universities, and its administrative buildings and numerous classrooms provided an ideal location to house not only students, but to serve as a camp for civilian prisoners of war.

But, to understand how Santo Tomas came to be designated and serve as an internment camp, I'd like to share a little history. Even prior to the bombing of Pearl Harbor, diplomatic relations between the United States and Japan had become strained. There was great concern among Americans, and business men of other nationalities living in the Philippines, that an out and out war was looming. As tensions increased, two committees—the American Coordinating Committee and the American Emergency Committee—were formed. Their purpose was to coordinate activities among various civilian organizations, the military presence in Manila, and the Red Cross. Knowing there would be a need to house civilians if they were taken from their homes and their businesses confiscated, these committees sought and were granted permission by the administration of the University of Santo Tomas, to use the buildings and grounds as an internment site if necessary. With the bombing of Pearl Harbor and Manila on December 8, 1941 (Philippine time), the scene was set. The invasion had begun.

On January 4, 1942, all Americans and others who might be considered enemies of the Japanese were rounded up and taken to Santo Tomas. On January 23, 1942, an official committee agreed that the Camp be known as the Santo Tomas Internment Camp, or STIC as it came to be called by the internees.

By the time our family arrived, the camp had a population of over three thousand people. Under the auspices of the Japanese, STIC was a well-organized community of citizens. With Japanese approval, internees' committees were formed to address all the various components of conglomerate living. Activities were established and regulated. An educational structure from kindergarten through adult classes and seminars was put in place. Recreation and entertainment opportunities helped keep up the morale of the internees. A "Little Theater Under the Stars" showed movies and featured musical productions. A food and finance committee worked with the Philippine Red Cross to organize the feeding of the prisoners. Religious services were allowed to be held.

How the administration of Santo Tomas functioned, evolved and changed during the three years of Japanese occupation is a story in and of itself. Many books have been written on the history of the STIC and the internet is loaded with information. It was like running a small city. In the beginning years there was an interaction between those inside the camp and those outside the camp. Those who had money in banks could access those funds. I know that our family had some money available to us, because Mother, in her precise manner, kept an accounting of our expenses: food (sometimes specific items, sometimes under the label of 'market'), school tuition, shoe repair, and so on.

My days were pretty much filled with the same kind of activities as those of many young nine-year olds might be. There were differences, of course. When we first came to STIC, Mother, Sharon (then four years old), Donnie (just turned two). and I were assigned to a women's dormitory where we each had our own small bed, sharing the space with many other women and children. I don't remember where we kept our meager belongings, under our mattress or under the bed, I suppose. We didn't have much. I don't know where Daddy slept during that time. There was also a men's dormitory and I presume that is where he was housed. We stood in a cafeteria-style chow line for our food.

70

My Life Defined...

School was held six days a week from 9:00 a.m. to 11:30 a.m. We didn't go to school on Sunday. I have two faded brown lined notebooks from those years. On the front of one is written Grade 4 and on the other Grade VI. We weren't issued text books. Our teachers would write on the blackboard and we would copy the material into our notebooks. Under the subject of Geography, I can barely make out my notes on the East Indies, and I can still see a fairly well hand-drawn map of that area with all the countries and oceans labeled. Examples of grammar, spelling (actually misspelling), arithmetic (fractions and percentages), and a history lesson are still faint on these pages.

I love this example of a history lesson that I composed as part of my sixth grade curriculum. It reads: *Who Am I? Instead of teaching in a school or building I spoke in a marketplace. My teaching was not education such as Arithmetic and Writing, but merely questions. I made the people aware of their ignorance and wanted to bring out the truth, justice and beauty. At last I was accused of corrupting the youth and sentenced to death. Who am I? (Socrates).*

Also in my notebook I had copied every verse of Henry Wadsworth Longfellow's poem, *Paul Revere's Ride.* I remember having to memorize it in its entirety. I also memorized long sections of *The Song of Hiawatha, The Village Blacksmith,* and stanzas from *Evangeline.* To this day I love to read poetry.

What do kids do when they're out of school? Play, of course. And that's just what I did. We played hopscotch and jumped rope. I was very limber and a great acrobat. I could do a handstand, arch my back, and bring my toes down to my nose. I could do all sorts of fancy cartwheels. Once, when I was taking my turn, probably showing off, another girl stole my *bakyas* (wooden flip-flops). I was so mad. Sometime later I saw the thief wearing them, my *bakyas.* When she slipped out of them to show off her stuff, I stole them back. In retrospect, I wonder why that incident is so important to me.

At some point in our internment we moved as a family to a *nipa* shanty on the grounds of the campus. These primitive shanties had sprung up early in the life of the camp, indicating a certain strata of economic wealth. They were laid out in the fashion of a small neighborhood, and each area had its own name. Ours was Area C, Section 17; our address was Shanty No.3, Beef Stew Lane. Here families could spend their days, away from the din of the crowds in the main buildings. In the early months of the camp the shanties were to be evacuated before 7:30 p.m. Eventually, men were allowed to sleep in them, and finally the Japanese administration allowed families to stay together. We still had to stand in the chow lines for our food, but we could bring it back to our shanty to eat our meals together. My brother Don told me the story of Daddy rigging up a makeshift fan that was worked by pumping a foot up and down to keep the flies off our food. Sharon remembers Mother taught her to read before she was old enough to be in school.

I also remember having a job. For ten cents a day, before the evening meal was being served, I would go to the nearby shanty of another family, gather up their metal meal containers, then go down to the main kitchen area, stand in line to get their allotment of food, and bring it back to their shanty. I don't recall how long this lasted.

Mother used pages of my notebook to keep brief notes: my brother and sister were given worm medicine; it worked. I came down with malaria and was put in the hospital with a fever of 104.4, and was given quinine injections three days in a row. I remember the songs we used to sing at night under our mosquito nets: *There's a Long, Long, Trail A-winding, Over There, Keep the Home Fires Burning,* and, of course, *God Bless America.* I still get tears in my eyes whenever I'm in a setting where the crowds stand and join together singing those familiar words which kept our spirits alive on those dark nights so many years ago.

Although I'm remembering life seeming rather normal for us children, I know it was not the same for my father and mother. The Japanese authorities remained concerned (and rightly so) about Filipino guerillas as well as Americans who were known to still be hiding in the mountains. Why my father was designated to go in search of these people, I don't know, but he was again, as when we were in Antipolo, sent out, this time with another man, to bring them (whoever "them" is, I don't know) in to Santo Tomas. In my notebook I find the notation, in Mother's writing, *"March 25—Paul left for outside."* Each day must have been heart-wrenching for Mother. Did she imagine herself as a thirty-three year old widow with three small children? Did she pray? One thing I know she didn't do: she didn't let on to us children any fear she might have had that our father was in danger. I'm sure I would have remembered.

It was almost two weeks after Paul left before Mother had any word of whether he was alive or dead. On April 6, in the little brown notebook, she wrote: *"Mr. Hampton arrived in camp."* Mr. Hampton must have contacted my mother because two days later, on April eighth, she wrote: *"Rec'd P.R. note."*

In my WWII file I found that note on a torn sheet of paper in Daddy's handwriting:

> *4–5–43*
> *Mrs. P. R. Crawford*
> *Sto. Tomas Internment Camp*

Pauline Crawford Crabb
Manila, PI

Dear Catherine:

Hope you are not worried because we have not returned, but we are O.K. and expect to be back in about two weeks' time. Hampton came in with us on the first trip, now we expect to get the rest with a very generous offer from the Captain. Love to all, Paul.

Pililla, Rizal

Pililla is a small town, about twenty miles from Manila and south of Antipolo, the town where we were briefly jailed before being taken to Santo Tomas. I have no idea of how a "Mr. Hampton" came into the picture. I couldn't find his name in Dad's notebook which has all the names and job titles of the men working at the Itogon when the war started. I couldn't find his name anywhere. Maybe it was a pseudonym. (These are the times I wish so desperately my parents were still alive so that I could ask them questions which would solve this puzzle.)

The final mention of Paul's excursion outside of the camp I found in Frederick H. Stevens' book, *Santo Tomas*. In a chronological listing of the events of 1943 he noted:

April 19—Twelve cables from United States addressed to Camp internees received through Japanese War Prisoners office, indicates receipt of cables sent from here.

Ralph W. Crosby and Paul R. Crawford return to Camp after accomplishing their mission of bringing in from the hills, back of Antipolo, four men and one woman.

What the report did not say is that my father returned to Camp with a broken foot. I don't remember the incident or my reaction to it while I was in Santo Tomas, but I learned the details from Bill Moule's book, *God's*

Arms Around Us. As I mentioned in an earlier chapter, Bill had worked for my father before the war, but the two families had taken separate routes out of Itogon and the Moule's were interned at Bilibid, another concentration camp not far from Santo Tomas.

Once the camps were liberated, Bill came over to STIC to check out the status of other families from Itogon and Baguio. In Bill's words, *"Crawford was given the same treatment that Harry received. He was sent out repeatedly to bring in other Americans. It got to the point where he was either going to get killed by the guerrillas or the Japs. One day he was waiting for the Japs to catch up so he took a chance on fixing things so he couldn't walk. He put his foot against a rock, then slammed a boulder on it. They made him walk back into town on his broken foot, but they let him go back to camp."* (p. 377) I believe that was the last time my father was sent out to bring those Americans still hiding in to Santo Tomas.

In the camp, days turned into weeks, weeks into months. The year 1943 came to an end and still the American troops had not arrived to rescue the prisoners. However, considering the circumstances, for most of us life in Santo Tomas continued in a reasonable fashion. According to Frederick H. Stevens, in his book, *Santo Tomas,* the first two years ended "with the camp in a much better condition than might be expected under the circumstances after two years of internment. Camp health among both the adults and children was good." (p.53) The Christmas season of 1943 was celebrated with Red Cross supplies reaching camp, pageants from sacred history, Handel's Oratorio "The Messiah" was sung by one hundred fifty internees, and the children received a visit from Santa Claus on Christmas afternoon.

Between January, 1944 and December, 1944

Gradually, or not so gradually, conditions in the camp became worse. As the war escalated in 1944, and the third year of internment for almost four thousand people began, the shortage of food became acute. Rations were cut. Red Cross supplies had not arrived. The structure of the camp took on a much more military aspect: adults stood for roll call twice a day, certain medical facilities formerly accessible to internees outside the camp were closed, no outsiders were allowed in camp. "...effective January 6, Camp has been placed under the direct supervision of the War Prisoners Department, the head of which is General Morimoto. Drastic changes expected shortly in Camp administration and operation," wrote Stevens. (p. 428)

Almost daily, in the written minutes of the internees' governing committee, there is some mention of food: the lack of food, the necessity to produce more food in the camp gardens, the quality of food brought into the camp (fish, greens, garlic greens) being in fair or poor condition. The general pastime for women was sharing and copying recipes that they were going to cook or bake once they got home. (It seems ironic to me, seventy years later, we still seem to be obsessed with sharing recipes. Only now it's done on cooking shows on TV, and internet websites.)

On April 27, 1944, Stevens noted, for the first time, "Camp placed under air raid alert at 3 P.M." To the adults of the camp it must have signaled hope that they were not going to be abandoned by the United States. Increasingly, the Japanese in authority were making more and more stringent regulations relating to the conduct of the internees. They also began to assign greater areas of the buildings, which had been previously used as dormitories, now to be used as hospital facilities as the number of sick increased, and more and more people were brought in from outside the camp. Mention of air raids alerts and blackouts become more frequent in the diary.

However, it was almost five months later, on September twenty-first, that the first U.S. planes raid Manila. By the time the air raid siren sounded at 9:30 that morning, "... large numbers of planes were already overhead. Bombing continues all day offering wonderful display of Allied air power, skill and daring. Japanese hopelessly outclassed." For the next three months the internees would hear and see American planes over the city, but it was not until December twenty-third, (my mother's thirty-fifth birthday) that, for the first time, B-29 superfortresses, four-engine bombers, the likes of which had never been seen before, flew over Santo Tomas.

A children's party was held on Christmas afternoon. Each child received one piece of candy. The better gift was given to the adults. From the skies a message was dropped by a lone plane into the camp: "The Command-in-Chief, the Officers and the men of the American Forces of Liberation in the Pacific wish their gallant allies, the People of the Philippines, all the blessings of Christmas and the realization of their fervent hopes for the New Year. Christmas, 1944". The additional gift from the Japanese was one extra hour before curfew: from 7:00 to 8:00 p.m.

Daily now, the air raids continued. The Commandant's office orders census lists in quintuplicate showing names and nationalities of internees, Camp serial numbers, sex, size, civil status and occupation. Restrictions are increased. Continuing was the focus on the distribution of food: to children, to the ill, and to those who were assigned physical labor. Families continued to exist somewhat as before, but with less and less physical activity.

Between January, 1945 and April, 1945

With bombings coming more regularly and becoming more intense, the adults in Santo Tomas must have kept wondering how much longer they could survive. Areas around the walls of the Camp were now considered out of bounds. It was obvious that the Japanese knew that the end of their occupation was in sight. On January sixth, over the loudspeaker system in camp came "a message from one of the Japanese staff wishing them goodbye and good luck." (p.476) Food was becoming even more scarce. Of eight death certificates issued this month, a camp doctor wrote 'malnutrition' on seven of them, and 'starvation' on the eighth. When he refused to alter the cause of death, as demanded by the Japanese authorities, he resigned as chief medical officer. (p. 481) Just when our formal schooling was discontinued I don't remember. My recall of these last days before our liberation is dim. Maybe there are other memories stored in the far recesses of my mind, but they haven't surfaced as I've been reading and writing about this period of my life.

My Life Defined...

By February first, the Japanese had killed and eaten all their *carabaos* (an animal related to the cow) and pigs. All the food from their gardens had been dug up or plucked from trees and packed on trucks. The guards were jittery. Fires were burning all around the city.

On February third, a number of American planes flew low over the Camp. They were low enough for one pilot to attach a message to his goggles and drop it into the camp. It read: "Roll out the barrel." It must have been thrilling for those who knew the lyrics of the song, as the next line goes "For the gang's all here."

At nine o'clock that night tanks of the First Cavalry Division smashed down the front gates of Santo Tomas and rolled up onto the plaza in front of the Main Building. The mood for most internees was jubilant, but for some time the tension continued as the Japanese had occupied the first two floors of the Education Building, fortifying themselves with machine guns and hand grenades. More than two hundred internees were trapped on the third floor. For two days food was passed in to the internees, most of which was taken by the Japanese.

On February fifth, the guards surrendered and were escorted to an area outside the camp. We thought we were truly free at last. But it was not so. Three days later the Japanese shelled the camp: fifteen internees were killed and over ninety wounded (p. 482). These attacks occurred for more than a week.

Perhaps this is how I came to have a memory of seeing a dismembered human hand lying in a street somewhere between the Education or Main Building and our shanty. No body lay nearby that I recall. Was it a time that I'd been standing in the chow line perhaps? I don't remember my having any trauma resulting from the experience, but over the years I have recalled the scene and wondered how it came to be.

Until very recently, actually until I began doing a little more in-depth research for my memoir, I had thought when Santo Tomas was liberated on February third, the war was over. The Japanese had been defeated. Far from it. The battle for Manila, one of the bloodiest battles of the war, actually lasted for almost a month with heavy casualties on both sides.

While some internees were repatriated within a couple of weeks, Mother's diary notes that our family remained in Santo Tomas for another six weeks. On March nineteenth, we were transported to the air field in Manila and flown on a C-47 to the island of Leyte, where former internees were housed in a camp setting near a beach. This is where we stayed for almost a month. On April sixteenth, we were transported to the former Dutch merchant ship MS Japara, which had been requisitioned by the Coast Guard in 1941 for military duty. Two days later we began a three-week zigzag crossing of the Pacific, headed back home to the United States.

All morning of that last day at sea, internees crowded the decks of the Japara, searching for landfall. As the sight of the Golden Gate Bridge came into view there were shouts of jubilation, tears of happiness mixed with anxiety, and many, many prayers of gratitude. We docked in San Francisco on May 9, 1945. I was eleven years old, Daddy was forty-one, Mother was thirty-five, my sister Sharon was six, and my brother Donnie not yet four.

Donnie Age 3   Sharon Age 6   Pauline Age 11

Chapter 9 ...by Joan's Story

The recounting of my life during World War II would not be complete had I not included the story of my dear friend, Joan Biason. As I wrote earlier, Joan and her mother and father did not come with the Itogon group of families when we fled to the sawmill at Lusod once we heard that the Japanese army was so close to Baguio. They took a different route. I would not see Joan again until eleven years later, in 1952, when I went to Wisconsin to spend the summer living with her and her family.

While in Santo Tomas, my parents had learned that Joan's mother was killed by the Japanese, but only after reading Joan's autobiography did I learn any of the details of her death. In her memoir, *My First 75 Years,* which Joan so kindly shared with me, and has allowed me to include here, she recounts the day her mother died:

> *In 1942 the Jap soldiers eventually arrived. On the day of our capture, my dad took us down the mountain following the creek. He had my mother and Betty [her father's stepsister] lie down with me in the middle. He covered us with what he hoped was a camouflage and*

returned to the creek. The Japs came running down the creek and shot at us—they must have already taken my dad prisoner. Betty was killed immediately. My mother called me to get the medical bag and to give her an ampoule—I don't know what it was. It was to be injected, but she broke the glass and swallowed the contents. I ran down the hill screaming at the soldiers. I don't know what I yelled. I did find my dad who had his hands bound behind him and blood on his forehead. Later I found a bullet had grazed my right side. I did not see my mother or Betty again.

In truth, I cannot imagine the grief and trauma that Joan and her father lived with in the days and years that followed. Her life was never the same. My family came home to the United States intact. We had no earthly possessions, but we had each other. Joan and I would be reunited seven years later.

Chapter 10 ...by the Idaho Years

Between 1945 and 1953

"And here we have Idaho, winning her way to fame.
Silver and gold in the sunlight blaze,
And romance lies in her name.
Singing, we're singing of you,
Ah, proudly too. All our lives thru,
We'll go singing, singing of you,
Singing of Idaho."

Written by McKinley Helm & Albert J. Tompkins
Composed by Sallie Hume-Douglas

So goes the chorus of the state song of Idaho. Although I lived in that state for only ten years, its influence seems to have infused itself into my inner being. Each time I return it is as though I'm connecting with some inner urge to be more than just a tourist for a few days. I want to belong. As I drive from the airport in Spokane, Washington to the Silver Valley of Idaho, through the tall pines and winding road of the Fourth of July Pass, I yearn to have the surroundings *be* a part of who I am. I'm sure the pull comes from the fact both of my parents spent most of their lives in the Silver State, and because my dad's ashes have been washed under the soil of the apple tree at his mother's farm in Careywood for almost fifty years now.

My memory is blurred as to how, in April of 1945, our family traveled from the port of San Francisco in California to Kellogg, Idaho. I recall that my father's brother Clarence (we called him CJ) and his wife, Sandy, who lived in Oakland at the time, met us as the MS Japara docked and we disembarked. We must have traveled by bus to Portland, Oregon as I know that we stopped for a day or two to visit with my Aunt Lillian, my father's older sister, her husband, Judd Addis, and their three children: Joyce, Myron, and Sara Mae. Dad's younger sister, Shirley, was also there to greet us at the neat brick house on Northeast Thirty-Third Street. From Portland we went on to Kellogg, Idaho.

Kellogg—1945-1946

It's hard for me to imagine the emotional homecoming that must have met us when we arrived at my Granny Ladd's small framed house at 716 South Division Street in Kellogg. Julie Weston, in her book *The Good Times Are All Gone Now: Life, Death, and Rebirth in An Idaho Mining Town,* called Kellogg "a one-horse town" (p.34), and having lived in the town since 1923, Ella Ladd and her family were well known. *The Kellogg Evening News* had printed the story of our arrival back in the States when we first arrived. Granny Ladd, Uncle Jack and Aunt Lois were especially happy to see my sister, Sharon, because her name had not been listed on the telegram sent to my grandmother by the war department, informing her the family was alive.

We were treated to celebrity status by the townspeople. I know this to be a fact because Aunt Lois told me, many years later, that she had mixed emotions about our arrival. Within a few weeks she would be graduating from high school with honors, and none of the spotlight was being focused in her direction. Lois had been accepted in the Cadet Nursing Corp program at the Sacred Heart School of Nursing in Spokane. In the fall, she left Kellogg to begin her studies. Her decision to pursue nursing came in response to her desire to do something toward the war effort, which was still being waged when she applied to the program. She had also worked in the shipyards in Portland, Oregon one summer during the war.

I imagine Granny Ladd and her mother, my Great-grandma Irwin, did their best to put a little meat on our scrawny bones, and Lois took me under her wing, often treating me to chocolate milkshakes at the Corner Drug. But Daddy was anxious to be reunited with his own mother, and within a week after arriving in Kellogg we left for Careywood to be reunited with Granny Scott and Dad's stepfather, Murray Scott. I remember riding from Kellogg in an old Ford coupe with a rumble seat where Sharon and I sat. Where this automobile came from I have no idea; we certainly could not have afforded to buy one at this point.

Careywood, then just a wide spot in the road on Hwy 95 between Coeur d'Alene and Sandpoint, boasted only a small store and post office. Just beyond the store we made a sharp right turn off the highway onto Blacktail Road, a narrow, rutted dirt road over which we drove another four miles up a hill until my Granny Scott's ranch came into view. It must have been a thrill for my father to see his mother's farm again. After all, he had been gone for nine years, and for the past four years, give or take a month or two, he had not been sure he would live to see his mother again. Sharon, Donnie and I were both anxious and excited as we'd never been on a farm before.

It was another happy reunion. As the war years had passed one after another, Granny Scott had not been sure she would ever see her son Paul and his family again. Dad's younger brother, Maurice, who lived not far away on another small ranch with his wife, Mae, and their three daughters, was also there. My cousin Mary Ann (who was called Mac) was two years younger than I and we became good friends. Her younger sisters, Shirley (who was called Bo) and Maureen (who was called Riley), were the ages of my sister and brother. They also welcomed us with open arms and fed us well. My Aunt Mae was a fantastic cook.

Whether we stayed at the ranch until it was time for Sharon and me to be enrolled in school or if we traversed the miles between Careywood and Kellogg back and forth all summer I'm not sure. Mac remembers Daddy being at the ranch, but not Mother and us kids. She told me he suffered from bouts of malaria several times, feverish and shivering so badly the sheets on the bed would be soaked with sweat, needing to be changed often. I don't remember any of the rest of us having any relapses after we got back to the States.

Later that summer, before the next school year began, my parents sent me, alone by bus, back to Portland to have my educational level evaluated. They didn't know how much I had missed by being in Santo Tomas, and were concerned about the appropriate grade level for me. I was to stay with Aunt Shirley. Aunt Lillian and Aunt Shirley owned a millinery shop: Shirley's Millinery, "East Portland's Exclusive Hat Shop," their business card read.

In a letter dated June 5, 1945, sitting in the shop, I typed:

Dear Daddy and all, I am here at Shirley's now. The bus got here about 9:30. I went inside and could not find Shirley at all. I got my box without any trouble. I went inside and saw Lillian and Shirley waiting for me.... All my love to a dearst [sic] *daddy. Mike*

Aunt Lillian added:

Pauline ...is a big girl. She got in a little ahead of time last night and she went and got her bag that she had checked and then came over to where we were waiting....She said she had a grand trip and she seemed very happy.

Four days later, I wrote:

...HERE COMES THE GOOD NEWS. I took an achievement test on Wednesday and Shirley phoned the superintendent of the school and she said my tests

My Life Defined...

say I'll be in The Seventh Grade. The superintendent [I'm wondering if she was actually the principal] *who is a Miss McGill said she thought I shouldn't go to summer school because I will be ahead of myself. Shirley phoned Daddy yesterday and I told him about it and he said I will not have to go to summer school but to stay a week or so and then come back to Idaho.*

When I got back to Kellogg, my parents had rented a house at 725 South Division Street, across the street and a couple of houses up the hill from Granny Ladd's.

By August, after helping with the haying on his mother's farm, my father had found work with the Idaho Bureau of Mines in Kellogg. However, he was always looking for something better, and 'something better' came along with an offer from the American Smelting and Refining Company to work in Ecuador, South America. By March, 1946, he had a new passport and a visa from the Republica del Ecuador with permission to work in that country.

The plan was for Paul to go check out the conditions and we would follow later. Catherine, with an ailing grandmother and a mother who had already missed most of her grandchildren's growing years, was not keen on taking her family to another foreign country so soon after returning to the States. This decision turned out to be wise because on July 4th, after a few days in the hospital, my great-grandmother died. Her funeral was held at St. Rita's Catholic Church and her body taken to Halfway, Oregon, to be buried in the family plot there.

On the first Tuesday after Labor Day, school began. Washington Junior High was housed in a building just down the street from where we were living and I could walk to school. Although my test scores were high enough for me to be placed at a higher grade level, Mother and Dad had decided I should be enrolled in the eighth grade, keeping me closer to the age of my classmates. It was a good decision. As it was, I was the youngest in my class and much less socially mature. In our class picture I'm seated in the front row, shoulders hunched forward with a sweet, innocent smile on my face. I'm not sure I was even very interested in boys. Further evidence of my immaturity was my resentment at having to wear nylon stockings to the eighth grade graduation exercises the following May.

Daddy missed my graduation because at the time he was still in Ecuador.

Scenes from my memories of that year in Kellogg include learning to swim at the YMCA "plunge", as we called their indoor swimming pool, spending long summer hours at the community outdoor pool, and working as an usherette at the Liberty Theater on Main Street where I wore a smart uniform of slacks, blouse and vest. When movie-goers came into the darkened theater after the show had started, I would hold my lighted flashlight low on the aisle and direct them to empty seats. After my shift was over I'd walk home imitating the roles of the actors I'd seen on the screen. Every Sunday Mother, Sharon, Don and I would walk the long three blocks from our house to Kellogg Avenue to attend Mass at St. Rita's Catholic Church. Later in the day we would have dinner at Granny Ladd's house.

For reasons unknown to me, when school was out Mother and we children did not follow Dad to South America. Before the end of the summer he had returned to Kellogg and had already lined up a job at the Triumph Mine in southern Idaho, working for his former boss at the Itogon Mine in the Philippines, Louis Robinson.

Triumph—1946-1950

In early September, after saying our goodbyes to Granny Ladd and Uncle Jack, we made the drive to southern Idaho. Daddy drove, with only a couple of pit stops, from Kellogg to Hailey, the town closest to the Triumph Mine. Nestled at the southern end of the Sawtooth Mountain chain, Hailey, the seat of Blaine County, was a small town with a population of about 1500 people at the time. Twelve miles north of Hailey is the town of Ketchum. A mile farther is the world-famous ski resort of Sun Valley.

We arrived in Hailey long after dark. To reach the community of Triumph from Hailey, Dad would have had to drive north six miles on Idaho Highway 75, then turn off the highway to the East Fork Road of the Wood River, and drive six more miles up a graded road to reach the mine. It was not a route to be driven at night if one was unfamiliar with the landscape.

We spent that night at the Hiawatha Hotel, the only hotel in town, situated just off Main Street. The next morning after breakfast, Daddy, Mother, my brother and sister drove the twelve miles up to our new home at Triumph, while I was given directions on how to reach the high school, only a few blocks away, where I should enroll as a freshman. They told me a bus from the mine would bring me home.

Looking back, I can't imagine my sending my daughter off to register in a new school by herself. Did they give me lunch money or did the hotel fix me a sack lunch?

In 1946, Hailey High School was housed in a two-story, cream-colored stucco building located on a small knoll, surrounded by a dirt road. In the basement were the furnace room and the music room. A gymnasium ran the length of the building along one side and a football field was a stone's throw from the front of the school. My Wolverine yearbook for that year has photos of only 146 students, forty in my freshman class.

I remember walking up the front steps, and opening a heavy door. I looked left and right for a sign to the office, then seeing a door to my right, I walked into the office, up to the long counter, and announced in a quiet voice, "I want to register for school."

"Where are your parents?" the school secretary asked.

"They've gone up to the Triumph where my father works. That's where we are going to live."

"Where did you come from?"

"Last year I went to school in Kellogg. I graduated from the eighth grade."

Somehow the necessary paperwork was processed and I was directed to the freshman homeroom. Later that day we all assembled in an auditorium where a really good-looking boy (in my estimation) sat down beside me. More than sixty years later I remember our first conversation.

"What's your moniker?" he said.

Moniker? I had no idea what that word meant. I didn't know what to say.

"Well, I guess I don't have one," I finally admitted, somewhat reluctantly, having no idea what he was asking.

He re-phrased the question. "What's your name?"

"Oh, my name's Pauline, but everyone calls me Mike. My daddy wanted a boy."

The good-looking boy's name was Lynn Rainey, and when we gather for reunions every ten years or so, I am sure to remind him of our first encounter at Hailey High School.

When classes were dismissed for the day, a bus from the Triumph, carrying the night shift workers up to the mine, made a stop in front of the school. Five or six students whose parents lived at Triumph joined me on the twelve-mile ride to the little community where I would live for the next four years.

* * * * *

Discovered in the 1880s, gold, silver, copper, zinc and lead were all ores dredged from the depths of the Triumph Mine. In 1929, the mine was the sixth largest producer of zinc in the state of Idaho, and to accommodate the men, many of them single, a large bunk and boarding house as well as a number of houses for families, were built on land adjacent to the mine. Most of the people who lived in the community were employed by the Mine. It was not unlike the little camp at Itogon where we had lived in the Philippines. Several of the families had also lived and worked in the islands.

93

On that first day of school, Mother was waiting for me as the bus driver let off the students at the base of the road leading up to the mine before he continued further up a hill to the mine operation. She and I walked a few minutes up the main road, past the boarding house on one side and small frame houses on the other. As we turned left at the corner, a short distance up a canyon, set apart from other mine housing, I could see a small one-story house situated on a flat of sagebrush between two low-lying hills. This was my new home.

Within a few weeks after our arrival, the small house was expanded from one to three bedrooms, and a garage was added in the back. The only bathroom had a tub and shower. Mother and we kids complained to Daddy that every time we took a bath we got an electric shock when we touched the faucets to turn the water off. Dad, who always showered at the mine after his shift, and changed from work clothes into his khakis before he came home, was skeptical. He stood at the edge of the tub and grabbed the handles but felt no tingling down his arm like we had. Sometime later, Dad got sick. Although he seldom missed work, this time he was sick enough to stay home and had to bathe in our little bathroom. Being in the tub and wet all over, just like we did, he experienced a big shock in the process of turning off the water. The next day an electrician and plumber from the mine were over to remedy the problem. No more shocking showers. Isn't it funny, the little incidents we remember?

I was happy to have my own small bedroom, while Don and Sharon shared another, and Mother and Dad slept in the third, larger bedroom. Daddy made a desk for me out of a one-by-eight board supported by two orange crates. From printed cotton fabric, Mother sewed some curtains, threaded them with string and hung them across the open shelves of the desk to dress it up a little and hide my clutter. I also acquired a small manual Smith-Corona typewriter, which held me in good stead for many years. (I remember sending my first story in to a Reader's Digest contest, only to receive my first rejection letter, with the explanation that this was a contest for adults and not for children. "But please try again another time," the letter read.) I decorated my walls with posters of movie stars, primarily my favorite, Guy Madison.

Daddy also built, or had a mine crew build, a narrow framed box-like enclosure along the length of the yard on the back side of our house, which we sprayed with water in the winter and used as our own ice skating rink. On the other side of the house, on the closest low-lying hill, he had the crew scalp a layer of soil from the surface, just wide enough to create a short ski run for all the kids in the camp. Although we had skis and Sun Valley was only twelve miles away, I never skied or ice-skated there. I presumed we just couldn't afford it.

My brother and sister went to school just a stone's throw from our house, in a mine-supported one-room, one-teacher schoolhouse where children in grades one through eight were taught each day. Their teacher's name was Mrs. Fisher. Her two sons rode the bus with me and a few others into Hailey each day.

While I was engrossed in my school activities, I remember life as being rather normal at home. I had a job on Saturday mornings cleaning a house for a woman whose husband was one of the bosses at the mine. I also babysat for a couple other families. In the evenings after Sharon and I, often harmonizing on favorite songs, washed and dried the dinner dishes, we went into the living room and did our homework. On the radio we followed the saga of "One Man's Family." I also had a small radio in my bedroom where I listened to "Your Hit Parade" on Friday nights.

Mom and Dad most often read. She always had a stack of books she'd checked out from the public library in Hailey, primarily enjoying historical fiction. I can still see my father, sitting in his chair, always with a cigarette held between the first two fingers on his right hand, and a ditch (bourbon and water) at his elbow. Sometimes Mother would work on her knitting, crocheting or some embroidery project.

At other times we played cards, the game of Spit being one of our favorites. Mother sometimes joined us. Spit is essentially a game of solitaire which can be played by two or more players, each with a deck of cards. Speed is the essential element, and we had ongoing competitions. (I've taught my grandchildren to play, and sometimes I can still beat them.)

Every night during the fishing season, Mother would have a sandwich ready for Daddy after he got home from work. He would pull on his fishing waders, go out to some spot along the river that flowed just a few minutes away, and cast his line until dark. We ate lots of fresh trout.

Mother played bridge with the women at Triumph, and occasionally she and Dad were partners in an evening game with other couples. I remember their going to Sun Valley to a mining convention one year.

Once in a while there was a dance down at the boarding house, and I was allowed to go with my friend, Nadine, whose father also worked at the mine. Daddy once told me that if I'd spend half as much energy working at home as I did at dancing, I'd get a lot more done. I don't ever remember seeing Dad and Mother at the boarding house dances.

Mother, Sharon and I regularly attended Sunday Mass at St. Charles' Church in Hailey, and Mother belonged to the Altar Society. Each summer when it became time for Dad's vacation we would drive north to Granny Scott's ranch and he would help with the hay harvest. Each time, as we approached the far end of Granny's front field, Daddy would stop the car and let us out. "Run and shout to your heart's content," he would say. Mother would spend some of her time in Kellogg and we kids divided our time between the two places.

* * * * *

I remember my high school years as happy ones. I especially liked being on the debate team with meets at home and at schools in other towns in the area. The topic for our senior year was: Resolved that the president of the United States be elected by the direct vote of the people. We even debated in front of the local Rotary Club on one occasion. I remember I never once won the first debate after lunch. Later in life, I learned that a speaker should always eat lightly before a public appearance.

I also liked to write, and was a member of Quill and Scroll. Enjoying acting, I became a member of the National Thespian Society, and had roles in our Junior and Senior class plays. (I recall Mother brought me into town for the night of one of the plays I was in, but instead of staying to see her budding actress, she went to see a movie.) I earned my role in the Junior class play because I somewhat successfully affected the cockney accent called for in the role for which I was trying out.

Both my parents had strict standards for me, Daddy even more so than Mother. When I had Bs on a report card, Dad would ask me why they weren't A's. I think Mother understood the yearnings of a young girl to be popular, yet stressed modesty as an important virtue. I can still hear her saying, as I was modeling a pair of shorts that I had sewn, "Oh, Mike, those are much too short." I only wore a light shade of lipstick at school and never at home. Dad understood brightly colored red lipstick to be the sign of a loose woman, as that is how women were viewed by the rough and tumble mining crowd he had grown up around. I would never have thought of drinking anything stronger than a soda.

Because I lived so far out of town, whenever there were dances and proms in the school gym, I would spend the night at the home of a girlfriend named Ina Mae Cutler, whose family was very kind to me. My dates would pick me up from her house and return me there after the dance.

For the traditional "Senior Sneak," our class went as far as Boise, several hours away in those years. We visited the *Idaho Statesman* building and observed how a newspaper comes into being every day. That night we stayed at the Idanha Hotel, wandering up and down the halls until the wee hours (or so I'm told). I am reminded of the good time we had each time I revisit the pages of my yearbook of that spring. *"Remember the Sneak"* was penned any number of times on the overleaf and back cover.

I was only sixteen when I graduated on May 19, 1950. Earlier in the month Mother and I had driven to Twin Falls, the closest small city for shopping, to buy me a graduation outfit. We chose a navy blue suit, with the jacket trimmed in pink. We found a light pink blouse to wear under the jacket. At our baccalaureate ceremony, I wore white gloves and a small brimmed navy blue hat to complete the ensemble. Perhaps Mother remembered her high school graduation when she was valedictorian when the spotlight was on her, and she wanted me to look especially nice. My grades, though not deplorable, didn't earn me any such distinction.

There are only thirty-six students pictured in our cap and gown graduation photo. During the ceremony I read the class prophecy, and was awarded the American Legion Certificate of School Award for all sorts of honorable characteristics. (I always thought the American Legion must have selected me because I had been a civilian prisoner of war not too many years before, and perhaps that's why they had also invited me to be Miss Liberty on the Fourth of July float the year before.) Although Mother and Dad never said much, I knew my parents were proud of me.

It was taken for granted that I would go to college. There was no "if" ever discussed, conversations only of the "where" I would go. Although Mother and Dad wanted me to enroll at the University of Idaho in Moscow, I pleaded to be allowed to go to Idaho State College at Pocatello, mostly, to tell the truth, because a boy I'd gone somewhat steady with in high school was already enrolled there. (Just the opposite of my daughter who refused to go to the school we preferred because a boy she had sometimes dated in high school was enrolled there and she didn't want to be anywhere near him. Isn't that poetic justice?) I won out, submitted an application, and was accepted at Idaho State College.

I was unaware, all during my years at Triumph, my father's health was deteriorating. Working underground year in and year out was taking its toll on his lungs. Neither of our parents talked about it, at least not in front of us children. We only knew that during one of our summer visits they had bought some land down the road from his mother's ranch in Careywood, and were planning to move there after I had graduated from high school.

Dad surely must have been somewhat anxious about leaving mining, the only occupation he knew, to try and make a living for his family as a farmer. In the evenings that he had been sitting reading while the rest of us were listening to the radio, he had been doing some research, reading *Gentleman Farmer,* and his plan was to raise sheep.

As the months toward graduation whittled down, one more change became evident in our house. Mother was pregnant. We were going to add a brother or sister to our family sometime in August. I hoped the baby would arrive on my birthday, August 21st. Daddy probably hoped he or she (and I'm sure he was hoping for another boy) would come on his birthday, August 27th.

Because Mother was "great with child," as they might say in an old English novel, my parents decided she would take the Greyhound bus to Kellogg, while Daddy would take us children with him in the new Jeep he had bought to use on the farm. At the end of May, pulling a small trailer, we made the trip north to the panhandle of Idaho. With today's roads, the trip from Triumph to Kellogg is a little over seven hours. Sixty years ago, it must have taken much longer, especially in a Jeep hauling a trailer. We drove north past Ketchum, up, up and up over the Galena Summit, a scary road even now. We passed through the town of Salmon where Mother's father was buried, and in a few more hours found ourselves in the state of Montana.

On the long ride, I don't remember playing the alphabet game or any of the other games that my husband and I, in later years, played with our children to while away the miles. I do remember Daddy calling out, as he drove after dark, "Moon, moon, come over on my side," and sure enough, as we turned a corner, there would be the moon. Little did I know this would be the last trip I would ever take with my father.

Shortly after we crossed from Montana into Idaho we connected with the I-90 West, which passes through the town of Kellogg. At Kellogg, Dad turned off the interstate onto Division Street which took us right up to Granny Ladd's house. Mother's bus arrived some time later and Daddy went down to the bus station to pick her up. We must have spent at least a night at Granny's before leaving for the farm, but knowing my father, he would have wanted to get going as soon as possible.

When we arrived in Careywood, the people renting our property had already planted the fields. We moved into the empty house, the first house my parents had ever owned. For the first time Dad would be harvesting his own crop. He also bought a couple of cows. He taught me to drive the tractor. I can still hear him yelling, "For God's sake, Mike, hit the brakes!" as I very nearly plowed through the back side of a shed where we kept the equipment.

Everyone helped with the outside chores in some small way. Everyone but Mother. Mother's time for delivering the baby was close at hand, and it would have been cumbersome for her to be out in the fields. But even beyond that, Mother did not want to live on a farm. She did not like living so far from neighbors. She refused to learn how to milk the cows. And, perhaps she was just overwhelmed, thinking of the responsibilities of raising another child. After all, she was forty years old.

I was too busy thinking about leaving for Pocatello, and college life, to remember much more about that summer except that on August nineteenth, at a small hospital in Spirit Lake, my sister Chris was born. Mother had picked out the name Christine Marie, but when the time came for the birth certificate to be filled out Daddy insisted that his new daughter be named after Mother, and so she became Catherine Christine Crawford. Mother thought it would be nice to call her Christie, and for the summer at least, that is what she was called. I'm not sure just when the 'Christie' was abbreviated to 'Chris.'

In late August, with a dorm room reserved at Graveley Hall on the campus of Idaho State College, a new Samsonite train case (a high school graduation present) and steamer trunk packed, wearing a Croton Aquamatic wristwatch with a sweeping second hand (necessary for nurse's training, also a graduation gift), and two blank checks pinned into my bra, I said goodbye to my sisters, brother, and mother. Daddy drove me to the train station in Spokane for the long ride south. We got my steamer trunk checked at the baggage window, and Daddy asked if I had enough spending money for food along the way. He gave me a hug and said to be sure to write as soon as I got to Pocatello.

Two remarks I remember my father making to me about this time. The first was his saying, "Mike, if you graduate from college, I'll give you a trip halfway around the world."

"Half way?" I asked, quizzically.

"You need to be smart enough to figure out how to get back home," was his reply.

The second was an admonition: "For God's sake, Mike, don't be a sheep." In other words, he wanted me to think for myself and not follow the crowd. Did he know he wanted me to take after him?

I was off to start a new phase in my life.

Pocatello—1950–1953

The following afternoon, the train pulled in to the station at Pocatello. No doubt I was more than a little nervous, but several taxis were lined up and after

103

claiming my luggage I nodded to a driver who helped me get my bags in the trunk of his cab.

"I need to go to Graveley Hall," I told him, assuming he'd know what I meant and where I needed to be delivered because there was only one women's dorm at Idaho State, which had fewer than 2,000 students at the time.

It was a short ride across the town to the ISC campus. The cab driver helped me haul my trunk up a few steps and into the lobby of the dorm. Whether I included a tip or not as I paid him I can't remember, but most likely not as this taxi ride was probably a first for me, except for the expensive ride I took to Itogon from the Maryknoll Convent when I was four years old.

Graveley Hall stood at the far edge of the campus, a three-story red brick building. I was assigned to Room 301, the first room at the top of the stairs in the south wing. My roommate, another freshman named Arlene, who came from a large high school in a nearby town, had already arrived. Several of Arlene's high school friends were also enrolling for the first time, but had been assigned to rooms on the north side of the building. Somehow she wasn't very thrilled to keep company with a little girl from the mining camp of Triumph. (Is that how she saw me or is that how I saw myself?) Within a few days she had moved closer to her friends, and for the first year, I had Room 301 all to myself.

The word 'overwhelmed' comes to mind when I think of my first few weeks as a college co-ed. I can still remember walking across the campus, in front of the Student Union building, to my room at Graveley Hall one afternoon, and realizing how much knowledge existed in the world I knew nothing about, and how much I had to learn. A close second state of mind can be described using the word 'naïve.' I didn't have the slightest clue that I could buy used books, and, with my list of required texts in hand I walked into the bookstore in the basement of the Student Union building, and cashed one of my two checks for close to, or over, a hundred dollars to buy books and supplies. In 1950, that was not small change. My parents never questioned me on that account, and I'm sure it took a chunk out of their bank account. By the next semester I was a little more savvy and knew which used books would suffice for the classes I was taking.

During my years at Idaho State, in the early fifties, the college, more than less, applied the principle of '*in loco parentis*' in regard to female students, with rules of behavior that nowadays would make Graveley seem like a convent. Every effort was made to assure parents their daughters were well looked after. We were required to sign out and sign in if we left the building after six o'clock in the evening. From Sunday through Thursday there was a ten o'clock curfew; on Fridays the hour was extended to 11:30 p.m., and on Saturdays we could linger until midnight. Or was it 12:30? Ten minutes before the doors were to be locked the lights on the outside foyer would begin to blink, car doors would slam, and many a girl and her boyfriend would rush up to the small sheltered entryway, trying to make time for a last kiss and embrace. The penalty for lateness was being "campused" for a designated period of time, depending upon the circumstances. Those girls who were campused were not allowed to go out after six, and not at all on weekends. (I'm afraid that happened to me at least once.)

A formal Sunday dinner was served each week at one o'clock. We were expected to dress "appropriately," no grungy jeans and definitely no shorts. Emily Post would certainly have been proud of us.

Mother had always wanted me to be a nurse, so nursing is the major I declared. But I barely passed chemistry that first semester, and sciences didn't grab my interest in the least. Besides, in that era nurses were only trained in hospital settings, and if I were to continue along that vein, I'd have to leave the campus. I was having too much fun. I began thinking of a Plan B.

Also in my first semester, I tried out for the cheerleading squad and, to my amazement, won a spot on the team. I fell in with a group of party girls, learned to smoke (although I seldom bought a pack of cigarettes) and drink beer at the Bomb Cellar, one of the most popular college hangouts. Dad's admonition about being a sheep went unheeded as I wanted to be a part of the crowd. At the end of my freshman year, my grade average was abysmally low.

After the summer back in Careywood, I returned to campus, and again settled into Room 301. This time I had a roommate named Cathy, and we got along famously. I continued to have fun, knew how to buy second-hand books, and changed my major to physical education and recreation. My grades improved.

I also got a job working in the men's dining hall. Sometimes I worked behind the counter, dishing up food from the hot trays. More often, I wrapped silverware at the end of the chow line, a great perspective from which to look over all the boys and young men who came through every meal. What a job.

With the new major, I began to take courses in the Education Department where, eventually, I found my niche. Psychology and sociology fascinated me, and in my junior year I declared Education to be my field of study. I also liked literature and drama – oh, and did I forget to say that I had a role in one of the Drama department's plays during my sophomore year?

My Life Defined...

During the seven years since leaving the Philippines, I had kept up a pen pal correspondence with Joan Biason, my friend from our days at Itogon. She was now living in Wisconsin with her father and stepmother and attending the University of Wisconsin at Madison. During our sophomore year, letters flew back and forth between Madison and Pocatello. In one of her letters, Joan suggested I come back to Wisconsin the following summer and we could get jobs together. That sounded like fun. I was eighteen, almost nineteen, and ready to spread my wings. We would live with her father and stepmother in Clinton, Wisconsin, a very small town at the southern edge of the state, not far from Chicago, Illinois. With an okay from my folks, I didn't go home. Instead, I got a ride with a member of the football team who was driving back to his home in Chicago. The only detail that remains from that trip is the first night I spent in Clinton.

Joan hadn't yet come home from the university. Her parents appeared as complete strangers to me since I had last seen her father in 1941, when I was only eight years old, and had never met Ruth, his second wife, who was very pregnant. They lived in an older two-story house with the bedrooms upstairs. In the middle of the night came a loud clashing of thunder and flashing of lightning like I had never experienced before. Rain poured down in heavy sheets on the roof just over my head. I huddled under my blankets, pulling them close around my shoulders, wondering what on earth I'd gotten myself in for. Never had I remembered such a storm in Idaho. Daylight did not come soon enough.

Joan arrived within a day or two, and we began getting reacquainted, remembering a few things from our childhood, but never really talking about our experiences during the war. Our personalities were very different.

Joan was very serious, very intellectual, and wanted to be a physician like her father, but had been discouraged by her advisors and was being channeled into a physical therapy major. I, on the other hand, wasn't sure just what I wanted to do as a career, but felt that teaching would be a safe and sure way to find a job.

Within a short time, probably through one of Doc's contacts, we found jobs on an assembly line at the Borg-Warner factory in nearby Geneva. For eight hours a day we placed silica gel capsules in the tops of 50 millimeter shells which came in plastic crates with twenty-five shells in each crate, sliding the crates down to the next function when we had completed our step of the task. For Joan it was incredibly boring. Each day at lunch we played bridge with another couple whose faces have faded from my memory. I, on the other hand, enjoyed talking and listening to the different personalities who shared our work space. One day I overheard this cute and saucy young woman named Delores talking to her friend. "I just love *fracturizing* with the boys," she said. I really laughed to myself. My world was expanding, and maybe 'fracturizing' was a better description than 'fraternizing.'

Shortly before it was time for me to return to Idaho, Joan and I went to Chicago for a weekend to visit a friend of her family who worked in a radio station there. With its tall buildings and hustling traffic, this was the largest city I had ever seen. As we arrived at our hotel, we stood in front of a tall door with glass panes and partitions, circling around and around. Joan stepped into a vacant partition and I jumped in right behind her. As our partition opened onto the lobby, Joan jumped out. So did I.

"Why did you do that?" she asked, exasperated with me.

"Do what?" I asked, shakily.

"Jump in with me."

I don't remember what I answered, but I had never seen a revolving door before and not being quite sure what to do, I just followed her lead.

Another first for me on that trip was a visit to the Chicago Public Library with its two large lions guarding the tall front doors. Apart from the college library where I went to study, the only libraries I had known were in Kellogg and Hailey. They were small buildings in which books were shelved in rows upon rows between narrow aisles. They had no great halls with masterpiece paintings upon the walls. No flights of stairs, no high ceilings. I'd seen nothing as wonderful as this.

On that same trip, without the distraction of our jobs and chores at home, Joan and I had long hours to talk. I mention this because I believe it was this give and take and sharing of ideas and dreams that drew us closer together as friends. We've now been friends for more than seventy years.

Before summer's end, Joan's stepmother had delivered a healthy baby boy whom they named Louis. Because I had a baby sister just two, another common interest, much younger siblings, was forged into the chain of our friendship.

In late August the time came for me to make the bus trip back to the 'real west', as one of my co-workers at the factory called the state of Idaho. I stopped in Dickinson, North Dakota to visit with a friend from Triumph, Madge Stefanatz, who had been my godmother at my Confirmation rite at St. Charles Church in Hailey. I spent the night at her home then continued my journey back to Idaho. I was only home a week or so before it was time to get back to Pocatello for my junior year at Idaho State.

Life was now not as exciting as it had been when I was a freshman and everything was new. I did not belong to any of the three sororities on campus, and my social life had diminished as new classes of newly graduated high school girls severely diluted the chances of junior and senior women finding a quick date. The boy I had dated in high school, and briefly dated at ISC, had joined the army during the summer. I spent most of my free time with a group of girlfriends. I resumed my job at the dining hall, now earning enough money to pay most of my college expenses.

At Christmastime, I took the bus home to Careywood, wanting to spend Christmas with my family, but hoping to come back and spend New Year's Eve in Ketchum, the small community (at that time) adjacent to Sun Valley, only twelve miles from where I had gone to high school. Ketchum, with its proximity to the ski resort was *the* place to be for New Year's Eve. 'Everyone' would be there. Before leaving campus, I had made arrangements with a friend to pick me up from the bus station in Pocatello and we'd drive up to Ketchum together.

But nature had other plans. The day before I was to leave snowflakes began drifting down from the skies. Before long the driveway and the fields were blanketed with a light coat of white fluff. By afternoon there was no more sign of the long driveway leading from the house to the main road. It snowed, and it snowed, and it snowed. Even on a big Greyhound bus, the highways would be dangerously icy. My hopes were dashed. I spent the rest of the Christmas holiday at home with the family. (I have yet to spend New Year's Eve in Ketchum, and at this late date it isn't even on my bucket list.)

The next semester began in the middle of January. Every new semester brought new faces to campus. I was anxious to see who might be crossing my station at the end of the chow line in the dining hall, picking up his silverware each meal. Often, at the beginning of a semester there were athletes, having had offers of scholarships, checking out the school. Quite a few came from out of state, mainly from California. There was some kind of mystique being from California, women as well as men having a sophistication, in my eyes, that seemed to put them on a higher plane than homegrown Idahoans.

One of these Californians I had come to know was Bob Blanton, a fellow on the ISC boxing team, who came from Pasadena. We had never dated, were just friends trading small talk whenever our paths crossed. Accompanying Bob along the chow line one evening was an older, but nice-looking guy I'd never seen before. For some reason I thought he might be a golfer.

When they got down to the end of the line, Bob said, "Mike, I'd like you to meet my friend, Dee Crabb. We went to school together in Pasadena." Then, turning his head away, he said, "Dee, this is Mike Crawford."

My exact response has long been forgotten, but I thought he had a nice smile. He definitely looked older than most of the "boys" I knew around campus. This look might have been earned since I soon learned he had recently been discharged from the army after spending time in Korea.

111

Not long after our first encounter, one Sunday, after the noon meal, Dee asked me if I'd like to go out with him and Bob and some of their friends for a picnic and bonfire at Ross Park, a gathering place close to the edge of the campus. Of that first date all I remember is the bon fire and drinking beer out of a fish bowl. Ah youth.

Whether he dated other girls or not after that I can't say. I only know that each time he came through the chow line he would take his tray to whatever table his friends were sitting, and position himself so he could look over and see me. I liked the attention. It was also convenient that he owned a car, a '46 four-door muscatel-red Dodge. We didn't have to double-date with someone else each time we went out.

Only a few months into the new semester, Dee received a telephone call from his half-brother Vernon. Dee's mother, living now in Banning, California, had had a stroke, Vernon told him. Dee didn't have enough money for a plane ticket and so took the next train to southern California. Sadly, before he arrived, she had died. When he got back to Pocatello, we spent many hours talking, sitting in his car in the parking lot of Graveley Hall before the lights started blinking for curfew. He talked about his mother, how she had raised him after his father died when Dee was only fourteen, how she had married again while he was in Korea and that he hadn't lived with her when he came home because she had moved from Pasadena. Instead, he had gone to stay with one of her closest friends from Missouri, a woman named Mae Sweeney. He told me more about the rest of his family in Pasadena, about Vernon and Edna and their four children. He told me about relatives in Kansas and Missouri. I was a good listener, and he was so dear.

I regularly wrote to my parents about (most of) my activities. I was fairly casual when I wrote that "Dee and I

112

went to the show," "Dee and I" did this or "Dee and I" did that.

One Sunday afternoon, shortly after the Spring break, Dee asked me if I'd like to ride up see the American Falls with him. He had asked one of the cooks in the dining hall to fix a picnic lunch for us. (Eating out in a fancy restaurant was way beyond his means.) From a photograph Dee took that day, I see I wore a white sleeveless print dress dotted with purple violets on its sheer fabric, and was gathered at the waist. (I had sewn it myself.) At the neckline I had pinned a small bunch of silk violets.

The town of American Falls is twenty-five miles east of Pocatello. A small lake is backed up by a dam which lets overflow water into a rushing stream that surges beneath a high trestle over which the Union Pacific railroad line crosses the water. Large ochre rocks line the stream. We got out of the car and climbed across the rocks, and settled ourselves down near the water.

We talked and talked and talked. My memory of the afternoon's conversation amounts to the most important question Dee asked of me. "Do you think we could make a go of it?"

He was going to college on the GI bill and there would be extra money if he were married. We could live in campus housing. In our dreamy scenario I would graduate first, get a teaching job—and then we'd have lots of money. After he graduated we would move to Pasadena, where he would get a job. His mother had left him a small Spanish-style house with a tall palm tree in the front yard, and a fig and apricot tree in the back yard. It sounded like a hacienda to me.

There was no ring for him to slip on my finger, but by the end of our little adventure that afternoon, we had a commitment to one another. We wanted to make a future together. He wanted me to come to California to meet Vernon and his family and Mae Sweeney. I told him I had to go home and tell my parents of our plans. I was more than a little nervous. My mother and father had never met this young man, four years older than I, who I wanted to spend the rest of my life with.

When we got back to the campus that evening many of our friends thought we'd gone off and eloped—such was their understanding of our serious relationship.

One of my stipulations to getting married was that I wanted to be married in a Catholic church. Dee, being raised a Methodist, would have to go through a series of instructions before we could be married. He told me his friend Anne Johnson was a Catholic and he would talk to her as soon as he got back to Pasadena. We didn't set any date for our wedding. I didn't know what was expected of me when I got back to the farm, or how my parents would react.

Somehow we got through the rest of the semester. Looking back, most of my studying consisted of staying up late the night before a test, smoking borrowed cigarettes to keep me awake, and cramming as much of the content of the course as I could into my head. Luckily, I passed all of my courses. Through the Education Department, arrangements were made for me to do my student teaching assignment at Pocatello High School in September. Dee would go back to Pasadena and work during the summer.

One of my girlfriends, Vicki Graves, who lived in Pocatello, offered to drive me home on the long trip north to Careywood. A postcard I wrote to Dee, dated June tenth, tells him that we took our time on the road, stopping first at a friend's home in Boise, where we spent the night, then drove north on the scenic route of Highway 55 toward McCall, which sits by a small, pristine lake where we stayed a second night before arriving at the ranch. Vicki spent two or three nights visiting at our place before she headed back to Pocatello.

After Vicki left, and because Daddy was living with Granny Ladd during the week, while working in one of the mines near there, Mother and I had a little time alone together, a time to talk. I got up the courage to tell her that Dee and I wanted to be married. "Married?" she asked me quizzically. "I thought, when you wrote in your letters about all the things you did with Dee, that 'Dee' was one of your girlfriends. I had a friend in the Philippines whose name was Delores and we all called her Dee." What a shock for Mom.

I listed all Dee's wonderful qualities, and showed Mother the photo he had given me, inscribed *"To Pauline, With all my love, Dee."* But she was rather quiet for the rest of our conversation. She had to absorb that bombshell.

That night I wrote Dee a lengthy letter. "When I told Mother I planned to get married, her only comment was, 'Oh?'" I continued, in a more sarcastic tone, "They sure care." And then, to reassure him, I added "...but seriously, everyone accepted the fact very well and there weren't even any objections when I said I was going to California this summer." (Had Mother remembered she had traveled to Las Vegas from Idaho, some twenty years earlier to marry my father?)

Every day I wrote a letter to Dee and made a trip to the store/post office out on the highway to check for an envelope from him. I still hadn't had a letter but wrote to him again on the thirteenth when I mentioned my father's reaction to the news I wanted to get married:

Daddy came home from the mine about 4:30 last night and was naturally curious about what I had to tell him—I didn't mention you in any letters before I came home. When I told him he wasn't too surprised. He asked all about you, etc. but this morning when I showed him your picture he said, 'Is this the pharmacist?' showing just how much attention he paid when I was talking to him. He has the least curiosity of anyone I know!

Farther along in the letter I added:

Haven't told Daddy about going to California. Don't think he will approve—but I'm coming anyway—only hope there won't be a scene.

Just when, after I had gone away to college, my father had started back working in a mine I'm not sure, but I suspect this decision came because he was not earning enough from the farm to keep his family afloat. While he was gone during the week, my younger sister and brother had the responsibility for the day-to-day running of the ranch, as we called the farm. I wrote to Dee, *"Sharon and Donnie get up in the mornings and do the milking and take care of the sheep. I just stay inside and help Mother. Am afraid I don't make a very good farmer's daughter."*

But just a couple of days after this letter was written, when Sharon was gone for a few days to stay with Granny Ladd in Kellogg, I was pressed into duty. *"...I've fallen heir to Sharon's chores,"* I wrote. *"This morning I helped Donnie with the milking, and this afternoon I took the sheep out to pasture. Think of that—a common sheepherder. But it was a nice afternoon and I enjoyed the solitude. I even saw a yearling deer. Do you remember what you said about wanting someone else with you to enjoy the scenery?"*

On the fifteenth, after anxiously watching almost two weeks for the mail each day, I finally got my first letter from Dee. It was mostly full of trivia about what he'd been doing since he got back to Pasadena. He was living at Mae Sweeney's house on East Orange Grove Blvd., a street name that still, in the many years since, brings warm memories to mind.

Dee asked if I could possible come to California by the end of the month so we could celebrate the Fourth of July together. He was so glad we took some pictures the day we went to American Falls: "*I look at them at least a dozen times a day.*"

I would love to have told him I'd be on the next train or bus headed south, but the road was not that smooth.

My mother is quite unhappy at the thought of my getting married this summer. Her objection is not to you, or the fact that I'd be married in California, but she is deathly afraid I won't finish school next June— pregnancy you know—and that is her heart's desire— to see me graduate. It doesn't do any good for me to talk to her as she only cries—nothing serious, but unpleasant. ...I haven't even told Daddy I was coming yet. Heaven only knows what he will say.

Our letters flew to each other every day. My parents kidded me, maybe forgetting how they had written longing letters so many years before.

In looking back, collectively, at the letters of that summer, I am amazed at how hard I worked while I was home. Although Daddy was working in Kellogg, we were still farming. We had over 70 sheep which my sister, brother and I had to take out to pasture every morning, sometimes as early as 4:00 a.m. We had cows which had to be milked, and we had an occasional ewe that brought forth a lamb. I also helped Mother in the house, cleaning, scrubbing floors and helping with dishes. And. according to my letters, I also had the sewing machine out, sewing a couple of skirts and blouses for school since I was all set to do my student teaching at Pocatello High School the next semester. Often my letters began with, "*Dear Dee, I am so tired tonight...*" Mother did not want to be a farmer's wife and never learned to milk the cows so that chore always fell to Don, Sharon and me that summer. (There's no procrastinating when the time comes to milk cows.) In Mom's defense, she did have a toddler to take care of, and she must have had some heart in the endeavor, as I wrote that she went to town and brought home a little piglet which Sharon named Posey. Perhaps this was a 4-H project for one of the kids.

The daily letters between Dee and me must have convinced my parents that I was definitely planning to go to Pasadena before the summer was out, not necessarily to get married, but to visit him and stay at Mrs. Sweeney's house. However, toward the end of June, Dee had started taking the instructions necessary before a non-Catholic may be married in a Catholic ceremony. His non-Catholic friend, Charlie Johnson, who had taken instructions before he married Anne, had introduced Dee to their parish priest. After work on Monday nights, Dee drove to the hall at Sts. Felicitas and Perpetua Catholic Church in San Marino to be instructed about the Catholic faith, and learn what was expected of him after marriage. Of one thing he was sure, he wrote me. He did not want to be converted. We had several exchanges of letters on that and other aspects of my religious beliefs, and I assured him it was not my motivation to have him give up his allegiance to the Hartzell Methodist Church which he had attended with his mother most of his life.

Whatever differences Dee may have had with the Catholic religion, he hadn't give up on his desire to have me join him in Pasadena. He cajoled me with the offer to send me whatever money it would take to buy a train or bus ticket. He had even checked on fares, he said, and in his letter of June twenty-fifth, was a money order for forty dollars, the price of a bus ticket from Spokane to Los Angeles on the Greyhound Bus Line.

118

Mother had told Daddy, probably early on, about my plans, and he had not told me I couldn't go. (I probably wouldn't have gone if my father had laid down the law to me.) It was decided I should wait until after Don and Sharon had gone to summer camp, because with Dad working away from the farm, there would be no one to tend to the sheep or milk the cows while they were gone. My parents didn't have enough money to hire someone to come in and take care of these responsibilities.

Mother, bless her heart, came around and began to accept my decision. "He's the goodest person I've ever met," I told her. "He seems like a wonderful person," she added as I would read her snippets from Dee's letters. She helped me get ready, not only for my trip to California, but also ready for my student-teaching assignment. We did more sewing. She gave me a home-permanent so my hair would look professional, and she took me into Sandpoint to renew my driver's license. She said she would ship the trunk with my school clothes to Pocatello at the end of the summer.

On a Sunday afternoon, July nineteenth, Daddy drove me to Granny Ladd's in Kellogg, where he lived during the week. Always short on words, Dad's admonition this time was, "For God's sake, Mike, don't let him make you quit school." It was still beyond his comprehension that we planned on my graduating and my getting a teaching position so Dee could continue his studies and earn his degree.

The next day I bought a bus ticket and at 2:13 p.m. boarded the Greyhound headed to Spokane, Washington, less than two hours away. Both Mom and Granny Ladd had given me a little money, so after doing some shopping, I went to a movie to while away the hours before it was time to board the bus. With both excitement and trepidation in my bones, I returned to the bus

119

station after the show and took a seat on a bus leaving at 11:45 p.m. for Portland. I'd made arrangements to visit Aunt Lillian in Portland for a couple of days, and she and Uncle Judd were waiting at the depot the next morning. From Portland I went on to Redding, California to say hello to Uncle CJ, before going on to Pasadena.

On Friday evening, sometime after five-thirty, because I'd made sure I would arrive after Dee had finished work, the long Greyhound pulled into the Los Angeles bus station. In my confirming phone call to Dee, I had said, "I'll meet you by the magazine rack." In my previous experience of bus stations there was only one magazine rack, and it was always situated near the ticket counter.

I was overwhelmed at the size of the Los Angeles bus station. So many magazine racks. Which one should I stand by? Perhaps I was also overwhelmed by the possibility that Dee might not be there to meet me. When his smiling face came around a corner, I breathed a huge sigh of relief. I'd made it. He really did love me. He really did want to be with me, and he wanted me to be with him.

Chapter 11 ...by the Boy from Kansas

Leon Dee Crabb

Who was the young man who sent me bus money to come to California to marry him? Who was this man my parents had never set eyes upon, and yet was to be their son-in-law? Who was this man I would spend the next forty-nine and a half years of my life living with? Who was, as he often called himself, 'the little boy from Kansas'?

Little did I know that day in the ISC men's dining hall, when I was introduced to Dee Crabb, this handsome young man with an engaging smile would one day, and in the not too distant future, be my husband. As we began dating I learned more about him.

On November 3, 1929, Leon D. Crabb was born to Leon Ezra Crabb and Bertha Mae Cave in McPherson, Kansas. His birth certificate lists him as 'Leon D', nothing more than 'D' for a middle name. He told me his parents were going to call him *LD,* but somehow that didn't stick, and since his dad was called *Lynn,* the Midwestern pronunciation of *Leon,* he became *Dee.* His baptismal certificate as well as his army discharge both list *Dee* as his middle name.

Earlier I wrote how my mother mistakenly thought the 'Dee' I mentioned in my letters was a girlfriend of mine. The name confusion continued for a long time, as at the time Dee and I first met I was still called 'Mike.' Often when we were introduced to new people as 'Dee and Mike,' they frequently assumed he was 'Mike' and I was 'Dee'. Little wonder when we became teachers we went by our given names, Leon and Pauline.

But back to the beginning... At the time of his birth Dee's parents were living on a farm outside of McPherson, in a small town named Holcomb, a town which made a dubious name for itself in 1959, as the location of the brutal murders of four members of the Clutter family on another farm nearby. It might have been forgotten had not Truman Capote, in 1966, written *In Cold Blood,* a book which became a best-seller, and later a movie.

In a letter to me from one of Dee's cousins, Eugene Crabb,[1] wrote: "*Uncle Leon had a farm, not in Holcomb, but in Elyria, Kansas, the hub of the farming community in the '20s, '30s, and early '40s.*" This might have been before Leon (Ezra) came to California, as records show that Dee's older half-brother, Vernon, was born in Elyria.

Elyria, at the time, had a hardware store across from a large grocery store, and three large grain elevators. Eugene remembers that his Uncle Leon was connected as manager of one of them. There was also a Bank of Elyria.

---

[1] Personal letter from Eugene Crabb, January 9, 2010

Eugene remembers:

...being fond of Uncle Leon and Aunt Bert, and later, L.D. They were cheerful, happy and real participants in their family and community associations. Uncle Leon had a nice farm house right near the town and farming acreage of probably 30 or more acres.

The family after supper often sat on the rambling porch around our rather large farm house and Uncle Leon was the best story teller of all. He told stories of his youth, especially riding horses with friends, and visiting the neighbors. One of Uncle Leon's expressions of amazement and surprise was, "I'll swan."

This expression was also remembered by another cousin, Harry Crabb. He remembers[2]:

Uncle Lynn was an excellent horseshoe pitcher and could beat almost anybody around here. We heard he was good out there [in California].

Eugene goes on to tell me more about life in Dee's early years.

Uncle Leon invested his financial future in a Western Kansas Sugar Beet venture that failed in the 'Dust Bowl' era; he was just unlucky when the drought

---

[2] Personal letter from Harry Crabb, January 16, 2010

brought on the Dust Bowl. I was in high school then, and it was a tough time for Western Kansas. The dust blew clear across the state, west to east.

Cousin Harry Crabb wrote:

I'll always remember Leon [referring to my husband] as an active child...He was a young kid (about five years old). Uncle Lynn had just finished milking their cow, bringing the bucket of milk to the house to strain and prepare it in a pitcher to place on the breakfast table, when young Leon stumbled and dropped the vessel on the dusty floor. Aunt Bert saved what she could, crying and apologizing for the situation.

Harry goes on:

I might mention the dust was circulating in the wind outside at the same time with no letup and all this made conditions so unbearable. We finished breakfast and returned home, a 4-5 hour drive leaving those folks to do what they could to stay alive.

Harry continues:

Their family gave up farming there to come stay with our farm for about a year while we all recovered from damage to our locality. Our crops were hurt too, but there was enough to make a go on the farm. President Roosevelt came out with the NRA (National Recovery Act). Farmers could apply for a 15 year loan at three and a half percent interest and stay on the farm, milking cows, raising chickens to maturity to lay eggs, raising sheep to have lambs for sale and finding jobs. The dust storms let up slowly. We survived. Please forgive me if I get carried away on my interpretation of the DUST BOWL DAYS. One had to live through them.

As I remember, my twin sister and I were hauled to and from school ¾ mile in Dad's grain wagon, tucked down under a blanket. There was dust everywhere the wind would blow – dust inside my building. But we only left our house as was needed. Our outdoor toilet was used very little. Instead our bed pan with handle was available. Just imagine the nights shaking the bed cover of the dust to enter a night's sleep. No storm windows. Most floors were always dusty. But we survived and Dad and Mom raised all eight of us kids to maturity.

Harry's memory of Dee being about five is probably right, as when Leon and Bert moved back to California, where they had both lived before and where they were married, Dee was enrolled in kindergarten at Hamilton School in Pasadena.

Just as I haven't learned much about Dee's father, Leon Ezra, in his younger days, I have little information about Dee's mother. She died before I had a chance to meet her and we never corresponded much with her relatives in Missouri. I know that she was born Bertha Mae Cave in Clay County, Missouri and was one of twelve children. Bert was a widow and, it's been my understanding that she was a distant cousin to Leon's first wife, Daisy, and had come to Pasadena to help take care of Daisy in her last illness. Daisy was buried at the Mountain View Cemetery in Altadena, California, and years later, Leon was interred next to her.

Bert and Leon were married in 1929, at the Mission Inn in Riverside, California. Whether they lived in California for some time afterward or moved immediately to the farm in Kansas, I'm not sure. Leon's son, Vernon, a young adult by this time, continued to live in the South Grand Oaks house in Pasadena where Leon and Daisy had lived.

When the "Dust Bowl" hit the Midwest, Leon and Bert moved back to Pasadena and shared a home with another family on Craig Street, not far from South Grand

Oaks Avenue. After Vernon and his wife, Edna, and their two young children, Eugene and Louise, bought a larger home a few blocks away on Parkwood, Bert, Leon and Dee moved into the house on South Grand Oaks. (Back in Pocatello, when Dee was telling me about where he grew up, I thought that 'South Grand Oaks' was such a magnificent sounding address and pictured a wide street lined with tall oaks.)

In our family album are several photos of Leon, Bert, and Dee standing alongside of Leon's older son, Vernon, and his wife, Edna, and their two young children, Gene and Louise, in front of the arched window in the small front yard on South Grand Oaks. From these pictures I see that Bert was a big-boned woman, standing taller than her husband. (Our daughter, Mary, has inherited some of Bert's physical attributes, even to her smile.)

Hamilton Elementary School, where Dee went to the first six grades, was located just one block from their house. When it came time to go to junior high school, Wilson Jr. High was an easy bike ride away. Dee belonged to a Boy Scout Troop through his church, Hartzell Methodist, which he and his mother faithfully attended all the while he lived at home. He played football in junior high and sang in the Pasadena Boys' Choir, a rather prestigious group at the time.

The Pasadena public school system had an unusual configuration in those years: 6-4-4. Following six years of elementary school, the junior high setting included the first two years of high school, and the last two years of high school were combined with the first two years of junior college, as what we now know as a community college was classified at that time. At PJC (Pasadena Junior College) Dee was a member of the gymnastics team and joined a local fraternity, Delta Sigma Rho, where he made some lifelong friends. He was a hit at parties as he and one of his buddies, Jim Blanton, had each taken up the banjo and enjoyed playing for their friends.

During his first year of high school, in 1943, when Dee was 14 years old, his father died. Although he never talked much about it, this must have been a difficult time. His half-brother Vernon taught him how to drive and arranged for him to get an emergency driver's license so he could work with Vernon in the summertime at Atwood and Purcell, a construction, cement, and paving company, which installed many of the curbs and gutters on the streets of Pasadena.

Whether it was before or following the death of Dee's father, Bert worked as a cook (and probably also served as a housekeeper) for a family who lived on South Orange Grove, a prestigious section of Orange Grove Boulevard in Pasadena. Because she worked during meal hours, Dee often had to cook for himself. (This proved advantageous when we got married, because although I thought I knew how to cook, having had the responsibility of fixing the evening meal once a week while I was in high school, I really was not very accomplished. He often saved the day.) He also often told me what a wonderful cook his mother had been. "My mother would have loved to have taught you to cook," he used to say in the early years of our marriage.

Following Dee's graduation from Pasadena Junior College in 1949, during the years of the Korean Conflict, he was drafted into the army and chose not to go into officers' training school. Following basic training at Camp Roberts in central California, he was sent to Korea. While he was overseas, Bert met and married George Mitchell and moved to his home in Los Angeles. She rented the house on South Grand Oaks to tenants.

When Dee returned from Korea (with the rank of corporal) he chose not to live with his mother and George, whom he had never met, but to stay with Mae Sweeney, his mom's closest friend from Missouri, who also lived in Pasadena. Being undecided about what he should do, he took his high school and junior college friend Bob Blanton's invitation to drive up to Pocatello, Idaho, to look over the campus of Idaho State College, where Bob was attending on a boxing scholarship. Dee liked what he saw of the small college, and after a quick trip back to Pasadena for a few belongings, including his banjo, he returned to enroll.

As I wrote earlier, one weekend, early in 1953, only a few months after the start of the new semester at ISC, Bert and George had gone with some friends of theirs to the desert near Palm Springs, where Bert suffered a massive stroke. Dee's brother Vernon had telephoned him and suggested he should come home immediately. Sadly, his mother had passed away before he arrived in southern California. Dee's deep sorrow and regret at not being able to say a final goodbye to her remained with him the rest of his life.

Shortly after Bert's death, George Mitchell took his own life. The two are buried together at the Forest Lawn Cemetery in Glendale, California.

While stationed in Korea, Dee was sent to Japan for a period of R&R, Rest and Recuperation. When he was in Tokyo he bought his mother a matching set of opalescent earrings and necklace.

On my dresser in San Clemente I have a small framed, black and white photo of Bert, most likely dressed for a special occasion because she's wearing an orchid corsage on a summer dress of eyelet fabric. She is also wearing the jewelry Dee had given her. She has a beautiful smile. I often say to her as I pass by the picture, "You did a good job, Bert. You raised a wonderful son. Thank you."

Leon Ezra and Bert Crabb raised a son I wanted to spend the rest of my life with.

Chapter 12 ...by the Summer of '53

At the huge Greyhound bus depot in Los Angeles, Dee had spied me standing wide-eyed by one of the many magazine racks and hurried over to give me a big hug and quick kiss. We picked up my suitcase, found the familiar muscatel-red Dodge, and started in the direction of Pasadena. It was not yet dark, and I was both tired and overwhelmed as we made our way from the bus station onto a freeway on-ramp. I had never been on a road called a "freeway" before and was amazed as all cars headed in one direction with a concrete barrier dividing the flow of traffic traveling in the opposite direction. In a short time the car was headed through the tunnels leading away from Los Angeles and toward Pasadena.

Dee exited the freeway at South Arroyo Boulevard, made a right at California, jogged left at Lake Avenue for several blocks, then turned right at San Pasqual, a street lined by large Spanish style two-storied homes, fronted by long, well-manicured lawns. Within a few more blocks he made a quick left turn onto South Grand Oaks Avenue. The houses on this street were not so grand, mostly single story, a combination of small, Spanish style stucco among a few wood-framed homes. Each had a small but well-kept yard, some with flowers lining a walkway leading to a front door.

Dee slowed and then stopped the car as we approached one of the smaller Spanish style houses with the numerals *240* mounted on the stuccoed archway that led to a front door. "This is my house," he said proudly to me. "This is where we lived when I grew up. This is where we can live when we move back to Pasadena."

A single tall palm tree stood in the yard with a few low shrubs planted in front of a tall arched window just behind them. Two taller cypress shrubs stood on either side of the window. Attached to the archway was a low wall which enclosed the area by the front door. Drawn drapes across the tall arched front window kept me from seeing inside the house. It was occupied by renters and we didn't disturb them.

This was certainly not the large Spanish hacienda with the fruit trees that I had conjured up in my mind's eye as we sat in the muscatel-red Dodge in the parking lot beside Graveley Hall. This was a small house. To be truthful, it was just as Dee had described it, trees and all. But it was a disappointment to me. I didn't let my feelings show, and I never told my husband about my first impressions of that house which was later to be our home for several years.

From Grand Oaks Avenue, Dee drove us up to Mae Sweeney's house, on East Orange Grove Boulevard, that historic street name which will always bring many fond memories to my mind whenever I think of Pasadena. (More about Orange Grove Boulevard later.) This, too, was a similarly small stucco house. It even had the same type of arched front window.

Mae Sweeney was a short, rotund woman, always with perfectly manicured nails. She and Dee's mother had been friends when they both lived in Missouri many years before. She greeted me warmly and took me under her wing immediately, making me feel like part of the family. I settled into her home nicely.

Most of the next month is a blur. The day after I arrived, Dee introduced me to Vernon, his wife, Edna, and their two younger children, Linda and John who were living at home. Their son, Eugene, was away in the navy, and their daughter, Louise, was still at UCLA. Vernon was many years older than Dee, and Dee was only a few years younger than Gene and Louise.

Dee had begun working for Vernon at Atwood and Purcell as soon as he returned from Pocatello the month before, and I soon found a job in a small factory on Santa Anita just south of Colorado in East Pasadena. I can't even recall what product was manufactured there. In the evenings after dinner we would go over to one of his friend's houses, either Rod Jennings's or Anne and Charlie's, and gradually I was able to put faces together with the names of the people Dee had talked about during the spring in Pocatello.

Getting married was uppermost on Dee's mind, and I don't think it took long to convince me that there wasn't any sense in waiting. Perhaps I knew in my heart that was the reason I had come to California. By this time he had finished taking the instructions required for non-Catholics prior to marriage to a Catholic, and we made an appointment for me to meet Father Arthur Lirette who would perform the ceremony and witness our vows at Saints Felicitas and Perpetua Church in San Marino.

We set the wedding date for Friday, August twenty-eighth, the last possible weekend before returning to classes in Pocatello. (We had to earn as much money as we could before we left since neither of us had a job.) I wrote to my parents with the details of our plans. After the wedding we would spend a quick weekend

132

honeymoon at Mae Sweeney's cottage in Surfside, then drive back to Pocatello where both of us would start our final semester before graduation. Mother replied that with Christie being so little, and Daddy away working in the mine, much as she would like, they couldn't leave the ranch. However, she suggested, perhaps her aunt and cousin, Edith and Evangeline Mentle, who lived in San Diego, could be there. I sent them an invitation, which they accepted, and on our wedding day, they drove up to San Marino, being the only family members representing the Crawfords on the bride's side of the church.

Mae had insisted that I have an engagement ring. I really wanted a plain gold band, but Dee said, and I can still hear his voice, "My wife is going to wear diamonds." Before too many days had elapsed, Mae drove me down to a jewelry store on Colorado Street owned by a family friend. There I tried on several sets of engagement and wedding rings. I remember feeling very uncomfortable about going ring-shopping without Dee, but now as I reflect on the time, I believe that I was not only the fiancé of Bert's son, but perhaps I was the daughter Mae never had. And surely Mae and Dee had discussed the topic of the cost of a ring ahead of time. Again I was overwhelmed, but within a week I was wearing a diamond engagement ring.

Dee asked his friend Rod Jennings to be the best man, and I asked the only Catholic person I knew, Anne Johnson, if she would be my matron of honor. Dee's brother, Vernon, agreed to walk me down the aisle. Charlie Johnson would take some pictures.

I didn't have anything suitable to wear as a wedding dress, and being very practical, I thought I should buy a new suit. My new friend Anne insisted we go look for a short white dress, since our wedding was to be quite informal. At the House of Nine (I can't believe I wore a size nine at the time.) we found a summery two-piece outfit which I thought looked as if it had been tailor-made just for me. It was a simple white pique, sleeveless, scoop-necked dress with a sheer white overdress, open in the front, fastened at the waist by a band of lace held by five fabric-covered buttons. At a nearby wedding shop we found a lace cap, edged with a row of small pearls. This was attached to a shoulder-length net veil. It was the perfect wedding ensemble for me. I've always been grateful to Anne for not letting me settle for a suit.

Anne also gave a bridal shower, and introduced me to more of Dee's friends. I was still somewhat intimidated by "California" girls, but by the time summer was over I had met most of their friends and felt much more comfortable.

Because tradition has it that the bride should not be seen by the groom before she walks down the aisle on her wedding day, Dee took his suit over to Rod Jenning's house the night before. He would dress there. I dressed at Mae's house and she drove me to the church on Huntington Drive. When we arrived, all of Dee's family was there, as were my mother's cousin and aunt. But no bridegroom.

In 1953, on the pages of a number of popular women's magazines, there appeared an ad for Listerine mouthwash. It pictured a little girl, probably four or five years old, dressed as a bride, sitting forlornly on the steps of a church, her little hands cupped under her chin, her little lips drooping sadly. That picture actually flashed through my mind. Had Dee gotten cold feet? Had there been an accident? Shortly the answer came: one or the other of the boys had forgotten something important (was it the ring?) at Rod's house, delaying them. Certainly delaying them longer than was comfortable for me. There would be a wedding after all.

Father Lirette had asked the church organist to play for our ceremony and, with Anne as my matron of honor, I nervously held on to Vernon's arm as we slowly walked up the aisle to the front of the church where the priest and Dee and Rod were waiting. Dee took my arm from Vernon, and later recalled my face being so pale and white he was afraid I was going to faint. We exchanged the traditional vows of the church, ending with the very formal "...and I pledge thee my troth." Within fifteen minutes we were outside again, now a married couple, being greeted by our small family and a few of Dee's friends.

With Rod at the wheel of Dee's Dodge, on which "JUST MARRIED" had been sprayed in shaving cream on the trunk, we rode back to Mae's house. In her tiny backyard lined with a few shade trees, our family and friends congratulated us. We cut our cake, served it with ice cream (which Mae had insisted upon), and were toasted with champagne.

We honeymooned over the weekend at Surfside, a private beach colony about an hour's drive down the coast from Pasadena, where Mae Sweeney and her late husband 'Sweeney' had bought a small frame cottage, not ten steps from the sandy beach, many years before. It was good of her to let us use her house as we certainly didn't have enough money to spend on a fancy hotel. A hotel of any sort, for that matter.

The downstairs of the cottage consisted of a front room about half the width of the twenty-five foot lot with a one-car garage taking up the remaining half. There was a small kitchen, with a bedroom and bath sandwiched in between the kitchen and a back porch which ran the width of the house. (We always had to enter the house from this porch when we'd been on the beach, so that we could shake the sand from our feet.) At the back of the narrow living room, five or six steps led up to a middle loft which had a double bed and dresser. Another few steps led up to a third floor running the length of the house, with barely enough height for a grown person to be able to stand up straight under its slanting roof. Here, several twin beds were set up. Quite a gang could sleep upstairs, and often in the past Dee and his friends had come to spend time here in the summer.

We ate our first meal as a married couple down the road a mile or two at a small place called Sam's Seafood Restaurant. After dinner, back at Surfside, we opened the bottle of champagne Dee had bought in a liquor store on our way down from Pasadena after the reception. Two cheap, shallow champagne glasses he had purchased at the same time served as our wine goblets on that night, and every anniversary afterward until our twenty-fifth anniversary, when we decided it was time for a pair of silver goblets. But to tell the truth, those silver goblets never quite held the magic of our two liquor-store purchases.

Beach cottage at Surfside

Chapter 13 ...by Life on Campus Drive

Between 1953 *and* 1955

We'd been married less than two weeks when it was time to resume our status as students at Idaho State College. At first we were a little self-conscious of the wedding rings we wore. Married students were a minority in 1953, and introducing Dee as 'my husband' seemed to trip up my tongue for a short while.

We were lucky enough to get into one of the married students' housing units on campus. Built for Navy V-12 trainees during WWII, these were rather aptly named the 'rabbit hutches.' Ours, #22 Campus Drive, first in a row or eight or ten attached units, was comprised of a living/sleeping area furnished with two twin beds (one of which we called the guest bed), a kitchen with a small table and two chairs, an ice box which required a huge chunk of ice at least twice a week, and a coal stove. On the very first day we called the little square box our 'home,' Dee used up every bit of the packing materials from our wedding gifts trying to get the coal in the kitchen stove to burn and stay lit.

Behind the living/sleeping area there was a postage-stamp size closet and a small bathroom. Water for a shower (or for washing dishes) was heated by a coal-fueled iron heater in a corner of the room. There was no hot water unless we stoked the heater with coal and the temperature of the room in the summer was often uncomfortably hot.

Despite the fact we were paying only $25 a month rent, the $110 a month Dee received as a veteran's allowance for education on the GI Bill wasn't stretching very far. We didn't get any financial help from my family, because my dad had told me once we were married, I was Dee's responsibility and it was up to us to make a go of it. Dee soon found a part-time job in the women's shoe department at Fargo's Department Store in downtown Pocatello.

We bought canned vegetables by the case and sometimes ate pancakes several times a week. Balancing a diet with meat, vegetables and fruit wasn't something I'd ever thought much about. Although I had been responsible for cooking dinner once a week when I was in high school, this experience somehow didn't transfer to being responsible for meals three times a day, week in and week out.

Despite my lack of cooking skills, we survived. My first pineapple upside down cake looked so beautifully browned when I took it out of the hot, coal-fueled oven, but when I turned it over onto a serving dish the batter, barely warm, ran down the side of the plate. I cried. And cried. I also burst into tears another night when I finally sat down to eat the mashed potatoes and gravy I'd served Dee. I took one bite and threw down my fork. "How could you have eaten this? It's awful." My dear husband hadn't wanted to complain and had choked down the whole serving of the floury, totally unpalatable gravy I'd cooked for him. Bless his heart, he was a good man. And one, it seems, with an iron stomach.

We each worked, sometimes consciously, sometimes unconsciously, at cementing our love for each other. We adapted to our circumstances and were happy at 22 Campus Drive. Looking back through the years, being independent and on our own helped us, I think, bond as a team. Many, many years, after one of the Olympic Games coined the term 'Team USA', we called ourselves 'Team Crabb'.

In early September I began my student teaching assignment at Pocatello High School, teaching a class in World History. Although Dee had been a business major up to this point, he so enjoyed helping me prepare my lesson plans during my stint at PHS, by spring he had changed his major, and we made plans to remain at Idaho State for another school year so he could complete the courses required for a degree in Education.

We had also put our names on a waiting list for one of the stand-alone housing units located closer to the campus, known as Senior Row. Although these were still ticky-tacky boxes, each had an actual bedroom with a door that could be closed. (Remember? We didn't even have a bedroom in our first place. It seemed luxurious.) Each unit had an electric stove and a real refrigerator. When the crop of graduating seniors vacated at the end of May, we were assigned to #210 Campus Drive. However, our rent went up. We now paid $40 per month, although the college continued to pay for all the utilities. We still didn't have a telephone. It didn't seem a necessity.

Pauline Crawford Crabb

When I graduated at the end of the spring semester, with a BA in Education and Social Science, my black graduation gown barely hid a bulging tummy, and my teaching career was to be put on hold for a while as we were expecting a baby in August. We had no grandparents who could help out, and in those years most young mothers didn't usually leave their infants in the care of others while they went off to work.

After graduation we made a quick road trip up to Careywood so my family could finally meet my husband. (I've often wondered what their first impression must have been. They sent me away as a teenager and I returned home married and ready to have a baby in a couple of months.) Both Mother and Dad liked Dee right away, and my brother and sisters had a chance to meet their new brother-in-law. Christie was growing up fast and charmed us both. I don't recall our staying long as Dee had to get back to his job at Fargo's. Making a trip back to Pasadena wasn't in the picture for this summer.

Almost all of the couples living on Senior Row were fairly newly married, and none of us had much money. We studied during the week and on the weekends three or four couples of us would gather at one of the units, have a pot luck dinner, drink a little beer or Thunderbird wine and play charades. On other weekends Dee would take his banjo down to the Bomb Cellar, the popular bar

140

close to campus, and he and his friend Bob McDonald would regale the college crowd with banjo-piano duets and lead in the singing of traditional, often bawdy, drinking songs.

One hot afternoon in August, as I was fixing dinner for us and LeRoy Cottom, a friend from school, my stomach began to cramp. Naïve me, how did I know these were labor pains? I'd never been through this before. When the cramps began to come at more frequent intervals I went to a neighbor's and called Dee at work. "Honey, I think you'd better come home. I think I'd better call Dr. Olsen." I hung up and called my obstetrician.

"How far apart are these pains, Mrs. Crabb?" Dr. Olsen asked. I had no idea. "You don't know? Time them and call me back."

Nervously, I timed them and called him back. "They're about five minutes apart."

"You'd better get up to the hospital, Mrs. Crabb. I'll meet you there."

I don't recall whatever happened to my dinner that night. LeRoy Cottom certainly didn't eat his dinner at our house. A few minutes past midnight, on August fifteenth, I delivered an eight-pound, two-ounce baby boy, his face a little miniature of his father. There was no denying his heritage. We named him Leon Paul after his father and both grandfathers. In a few weeks he was baptized at St. Anthony's Catholic Church where I'd been attending Mass ever since arriving in Pocatello.

We were not the only couple with new babies that summer and fall, and while our husbands were occupied in classrooms, in labs and in the library, we young moms spent our time doing what most young mothers did in those days: washing diapers, hanging them on the lines to dry, and "keeping house." Maybe I should have said "sweeping house." We didn't own a vacuum cleaner. Now when we got together on weekends, we'd put all the babies on one of the beds and hope they'd all stay asleep while we enjoyed playing our charades.

Dee and I did not go back to Pasadena to celebrate Christmas that winter. Instead, we made plans for me and the baby to go visit my parents after the first of the year. Not only did I want my parents to meet their first grandchild, but Mother had asked me to come at that time because she was expecting her fifth child in January. I was to have another brother or sister, and my parents thought I could stay at the house with my other siblings while Mother was in the hospital. Baby Leon, now five months old, and I made the trip to Careywood by Greyhound bus. On January twentieth, Mother delivered a healthy baby girl whom they named Therese Marie. (Mom's favorite saint was St. Therese of Lisieux, and her new daughter was named for her.) Memory eludes me as to how quickly they came to call the baby Terry, but she never remembers being called Therese. By the family or anyone else.

* * * * *

Dee was happy he had made the decision to choose education, not business, as a career, and moved forward with plans to complete the required student-teaching course in the spring, and graduate in May. His plan was to teach at the junior or senior high school level. In January, at the start of the spring semester, he was assigned as a student teacher at Franklin Junior High School. He had found his niche.

142

Several months before Dee's graduation, Harold Brinley, an assistant superintendent from the Las Vegas School District in Clark County, Nevada, arrived in Pocatello on a recruiting trip for teachers for the upcoming school year. He found several willing takers, among them my husband. Dee was offered a higher annual salary than his master teacher was making after more than fifteen years of experience in the Pocatello school system.

There was a caution attached to the offer. Mr. Brinley told Dee the cost of living was high in Las Vegas, and we'd probably have to make some concessions in our standard of living. Concessions? What concessions? We were currently living on $140 a month from the GI Bill and whatever extra Dee could make at Fargo's. (We didn't have much money but I had two pair of really good-looking, high-end fashion shoes.) Living on Senior Row, our expenses were few. The $282 a month salary he would be getting sounded like a windfall.

With his mother no longer living, Dee felt no strong urge to settle down in Pasadena. And, as I learned through the many years we were married, my husband had an underlying sense of adventure. We talked it over very briefly and the deed was done. He signed a one-year contract. We looked forward to a new stage of our married lives.

Although we had an almost one-year-old child, our life at Idaho State still held many of the characteristics of single life: going to football and basketball games, attending the boxing matches (Idaho State had a nationally well-known, highly-ranked team at the time), pot luck dinners and charade games with our neighbors on weekends. Dee still found time to play banjo and piano with Bob MacDonald at the Bomb Cellar. We were poor, but we didn't *think* poor.

In early June, with Dee's Bachelor of Arts Degree in Business and Education in hand, a contract to teach eighth grade in the fall, we packed the old muscatel-red Dodge for our journey back to Pasadena where he had a summer job waiting before we moved to Las Vegas.

It was hard saying good-bye to our college friends, particularly because we were leaving Idaho, and didn't know if or when we'd see them again. The camaraderie of a life-style of school and parties, common poverty, had forged a special bond among us.

One of these friends was Hatch Barrett, who with his wife, Claire, had become part of our married couples' social life. Hatch showed up at our place as we were packing our car, getting ready to leave Pocatello the next day. He took several long looks at the sad old Dodge, the trunk and back seat piled high with the baby's crib and high chair, assorted boxes of books, a couple of suitcases and Dee's banjo. The words "JUST MARRIED," sprayed on with shaving cream by our friends on our wedding day, had faded, but now were permanently etched into the rusting paint on the lid of the trunk.

"That old thing is never going to make it all the way to California," Hatch said.

Hatch just happened to have a part-time job selling used cars. "Come on down to the lot and I'll fix you up with something newer."

And that's how we happened to leave Pocatello early the next day driving a 1950 apple-green four-door Plymouth. We aimed to drive straight through to Pasadena, stopping only for the combination of pumping gas, quick bathroom breaks and snack food. But as we crossed from Idaho into the Nevada desert the temperature rose. Our new car was not equipped with air-conditioning, and we had to stop periodically at a gas station or at a side-of-the-road diner to fill little Leon's bottle with ice cubes. By the time we got back to the car they would have melted. The heat was stifling.

We took turns driving. As the daylight turned to dusk Dee took the wheel and turned on the car lights. In 1955 there wasn't much traffic on the highway as we sped along, but not long after seeing a Nevada Highway Patrol car parked on the side of the road, Dee noticed the black-and-white had made a U-turn and slowed down as it came up behind us, flashing its red lights.

We pulled over. But we were in a dilemma. The Plymouth had Idaho license plates. Dee didn't have an Idaho driver's license and his California license had expired. He had planned to renew his license, as well as change the registration on the car from Idaho to California as soon as we got back to Pasadena. I was the only one who had a valid driver's license for Idaho.

Before the patrolman could get out of his car, Dee, quick-thinking, said to me, "Get over here, I don't have a license," and as he slid across the seat to the passenger's side, I slid over his lap into the driver's seat. The patrolman walked up to the driver's window. I looked up at him.

"Your registration and license, please," he requested in a firm voice.

I handed him both. He looked at the temporary car license, then at my driver's license. He bent down and stared at us through the open window with a puzzled look. The trouble was that the temporary registration for the car was under the name of Leon Crabb, and my driver's license read "Pauline Crawford." He saw the baby in the back seat, and we explained that we'd just graduated from college, had only bought the car yesterday, and were going home to Pasadena. We told him we would register the car in California as soon as we got home.

He paused a few seconds, although it seemed minutes to us, and then said, "The reason I stopped you is that one of your headlights is way out of alignment. You'd better stop at the next gas station and have it adjusted before you go much farther." With that he turned, got back into his patrol car and drove off. I wonder what went through his head, and what kind of a story he told the boys back at the station that night. We only knew we were grateful he hadn't given us a ticket, because we barely had enough money to make it to the next payday.

We drove straight through to Pasadena, again pausing only long enough for the necessary gas and restroom stops, and to grab a couple of quick bites to eat.

Vernon and Edna had generously offered to let us stay with them at 326 South Parkwood Avenue, and almost without a break Dee, once again, went to work for Vernon at Atwood and Purcell. For the rest of the summer he dug ditches and poured cement for curb and gutters for many of the streets of Pasadena.

Chapter 14 ...by a Year in Las Vegas

Between 1955 and 1956

Toward the end of August we made a quick trip to Las Vegas to find a place to live for the coming school year. What a shock. We were so naïve. Even though we'd been warned, we had no idea how high the rent prices would be. Although Mr. Brinley had tried to prepare us, we were more than a little overwhelmed. Even in 1955, when Las Vegas had only a few downtown hotels and casinos and The Strip was on the outskirts of town, the cost of living was high.

Not too far off the main drag, on a sloping street, we found a small, unfurnished, one bedroom apartment built into the basement of our landlord's house, and we paid our first month's rent—$140.00. We were confident this would fit into our budget once we got a paycheck and knew exactly how much Leon would be bringing home each month.

Back in Pasadena it had been fun thumbing through newspaper ads, looking for the barest necessities in the Used Furniture section of the Star-News. We found a bed, and also a yellow Formica and chrome dining table with four chairs. The apartment came with a stove and refrigerator. No washer or dryer.

Dee worked at Atwood and Purcell up to the last Friday before school meetings were scheduled in Las Vegas. The next day, we loaded a small trailer with all our belongings, put Little Leon, now a year-old, into a car seat between us, and set off in the apple-green Plymouth for our new home and new life. We were going to be a real family. Especially because we had another baby on the way.

Before the next month's rent was due, Leon had received his first paycheck. After taxes and deductions the amount came to $282.00. After paying the rent, we would have only $142.00 to last until the next month. We had a car payment of $50, a tire payment of $12.00, and an $8.50 per month payment for a set of Collier's Encyclopedias. (Back in Pocatello a door-to-door salesman—and a very good one, I might add—had come around one Saturday morning. When my husband told him we couldn't afford a set of encyclopedias, he asked, "Do you smoke?" "Yes." "Do you spend twenty-five cents a day on cigarettes?" "Well, yes." "Then you can surely afford this wonderful set of encyclopedias. They will last for years." And that's how it happened. Those encyclopedias did indeed grace the shelves of our homes for more than forty-five years.)

Even with a small rent check coming in from our house on South Grand Oaks in Pasadena to supplement our income, it was obvious we weren't going to be able to stay where we were. Again we searched through Houses for Rent ads. Before the next month's rent was due we had found a small two-bedroom house on a dirt road named Goldfield in North Las Vegas. We shared a driveway with a smaller house on the rear of the lot where a middle-aged couple, Larry and Inez, lived. The rent for the house on Goldfield was $110.00 a month. We thought we could squeak by. I remember walking down Fremont Street, Las Vegas' main thoroughfare in those days, and looking in at the gamblers around the casino tables, wishing I could ask for just one of those twenty-dollar chips piled by the sides of their elbows as they peeked under their cards and pondered their bets. Instead of taking in the shows on the strip, Dee and I spent our evenings, after the baby was put to bed and any school-related tasks were done, sitting at our dining room table playing cards, usually cribbage, and listening to *One Man's Family* on the radio.

Although not the mega-entertainment city it is now, in 1955 and 1956, Las Vegas was famous for The Strip, then located a fair distance from the downtown businesses. It boasted such headliners as Frank Sinatra, Wayne Newton, Lena Horne, Peggy Lee, Joe E. Lewis, and a new up-and-coming musical talent named Elvis Presley.

However, the only two times Dee and I ventured down to The Strip were when friends from Pasadena came to visit. I can still see Lena Horne standing on stage at the Sands, her arms extended and her hands, with their slender long fingers gracefully cupped, beckoning to the audience. I remember being mesmerized by her beauty and her haunting voice.

We didn't drive back to Pasadena for Christmas, and I don't remember what I cooked for a Christmas dinner. My only memory of that holiday is when Dee and I woke up on Christmas morning, Little Leon had crawled over the rail of his crib, gone over to the Christmas tree, and pulled every ornament he could reach out of its wire loop hanger and laid them all around the foot of the tree. It took us forever to find all the hangers and replace the ornaments.

Another reason for not spending Leon's hard-earned salary on a trip to Pasadena was because we had a doctor's fee to pay to Dr. Emil Cava, our obstetrician. We expected our baby in late March or early April. However, mid-morning on Thursday, the ninth of February, I realized that something very different was going on with my unborn baby. I began to have pains in my stomach, and I began to spot blood. (Naïve me: I'd been in la-la land when my water broke with my first baby, thought this was the way it happened.) Leon had already left for school, but I knew I needed to get in touch with him as soon as possible. We still couldn't afford a telephone, so I made my way down the driveway and knocked at Larry and Inez's kitchen door. Luckily, Inez was home.

"Inez, please call the school and have Leon come home as soon as possible. I think I'm having the baby."

I went back into the house, got into the empty bathtub as it became obvious to me this was more than just leaking water, and I waited. Leon arrived shortly, and from Inez's phone he called Dr. Cava who gave him orders to get me to the hospital ASAP. Inez offered to take care of Little Leon, and within a few minutes we were in the car and on our way. Dr. Cava was waiting for us, and took me right into the delivery room. *Placenta previa* was the cause of my early labor, and within a few hours our baby son was born, six to eight weeks early. He weighed four pounds, fifteen ounces, and was quickly whisked away in an incubator. Neither of us had had a chance to hold our newborn child.

"If he makes it through the next twenty-four hours, it should be all right," the doctor told us. Dread filled our hearts, but I don't remember crying. We named him Laurence Eugene. The Eugene was after Vernon's son, Eugene.

My Life Defined...

Within the next twenty-four hours, I was discharged, but preemies were not released to go home from this hospital until they weighed five and a half pounds. Every day when Dee got home from school we went back to the hospital to visit Larry, as we had decided to call him. At first we were only able to observe him in his incubator; later in a little crib, when at last we were able to touch and hold him. After ten days he had gained the requisite number of ounces to bring his weight up to five and a half pounds, and we were allowed to bring him home. I've often thought how strong my baby must have been, to have kept going without knowing the warmth of his parents' bodies those first few days of his life.

As soon as I was discharged from the hospital, we had stopped at a pharmacy on our way home and bought a breast pump. For each of those ten days I pumped my breasts, hoping to nurse the baby when he came home. I kept that milk flowing. Also, not expecting the baby for six or eight weeks more, we had nothing prepared at home: no bassinet and certainly no little shirts or diapers that would fit a preemie. Yet even the Size 00 shirts that we bought wrapped around the baby twice.

Once Larry was home we would sit by the side of the bassinet, peering over the edge, just to watch the chest of the little bundle wrapped in blankets rise and fall; we needed constant reassurance that he was still breathing. Worried that he wasn't getting enough nourishment from my breast milk, we first supplemented his nursing with milk from a bottle. Still not sure he was getting enough nourishment, I discontinued nursing altogether.

We needn't have worried. Larry flourished. But we had had enough of Las Vegas. By the last day of the school year in May, we had our apple-green Plymouth and a small trailer loaded with all our earthly belongings, and our growing family headed back to Pasadena.

151

Pauline Crawford Crabb

Baby Larry

Chapter 15 ...by Life in Pasadena

"Home in Pasadena"
Oh, you railway station, oh you Pullman train!
There's my reservation
For my destination,
Far beyond the western plains
To see my home in Pasadena

Home where grass is greener
Where honeybees
Hum melodies,
And orange trees scent the breeze.

I'm gonna be a home-sweet-homer
And right there I'll settle down
Beneath the palms
In someone's arms
In Pasadena town.
      Harry Warren, 1923

"How did a little girl from the panhandle of Idaho end up living in Pasadena, California for forty-six years?" I ask myself. Easy answer. You marry a boy from

Pasadena and he takes you home with him. "Home in Pasadena," Harry Warren's song, recorded by Al Jolson, fits my image of Pasadena to this day. There we settled down "beneath the palms." Every verse rings true to the pride I feel whenever I tell someone I used to live in Pasadena. More than fifty years later, I can't think of a better place to have raised a family.

Ten months of living in Las Vegas was time enough for us to know that we did not want to call that city *home* for our family. The environment in which we lived, our house on a dirt road, the desert cockroaches in the kitchen, the clanging of slot machines in every store we entered, the trauma of our new baby's birth: all this made it easy for Leon to say, "No thank-you," to another year's contract with the Las Vegas school system.

Vernon and Edna, always looking out for us, were gracious enough to once again let us stay with them in their home on South Parkwood until the house my husband had inherited on South Grand Oaks was vacated by the renters who had been living there while we were in Idaho and Nevada. Vernon also saw to it that Dee was hired again for the summer at Atwood and Purcell. The next challenge was to find permanent employment as a teacher in the fall.

We were still staying on Parkwood when Dee was granted an interview with the San Gabriel School District's teachers' hiring committee. He got up that morning, showered, put on his one and only suit, and drove the few miles to the district office where two or three administrators interviewed him. One of those on the panel was Mrs. Dorothea Gibson, the Assistant Superintendent for Curriculum. After the usual questions were asked and answered, and the interview seemed to have come to a conclusion, Mrs. Gibson, a very dignified woman, who had been looking quizzically at my husband all during the interview, asked, "Mr. Crabb, is there a reason you didn't shave this morning?" Dee automatically slapped his right hand to his chin, shocked that in his anxiety to get to the interview on time he, who never missed a day shaving in his life, had forgotten to shave. I don't recall his reply, but the situation didn't seem to be a stumbling block because within the week he had been offered a position as an eighth grade teacher in the fall at Washington School.

As I wrote, many chapters ago, there was often a confusion of names when my husband and I were introduced as 'Dee' and 'Mike', our newest acquaintance often assuming he (Dee) was 'Mike' and I was 'Dee'. After our move to Pasadena, although family and old friends still called us by our childhood names, gradually, or not so gradually, when Leon became a teacher, and I was making new friends, we began to introduce ourselves as 'Leon' and 'Pauline'. (To eliminate some of the confusion, in writing this story of mine, I'll often refer to our son as 'Son Leon'. (If this were a text message or an email to all my readers, I'd print a happy face right here.)

Between 1956 and 1959

When we settled into 240 South Grand Oaks Avenue in the summer of 1956, Dee felt he was truly home. The little two-bedroom house he had grown up in was just right for our family with two boys: a toddler and a four-month old baby. Our next-door neighbors to the north of us were an elderly couple, Ed and Ella Barber. Ella had been a friend of his mother and father during the time Dee was growing up. Down the street lived another young couple, John and Jane Campbell, with whom Dee had gone to school. Anne and Charlie Johnson, Dee's very close friends, lived only a few miles away. Vernon and

Edna were only eight blocks away. Mae Sweeney still lived up on East Orange Grove Boulevard. Although neither of us had parents close by, we were surrounded by familiar and familial ties. I attended Mass at St. Philip's Church on Hill Street and registered as a parishioner. I was beginning to belong to the community.

But, because we were basically on our own, we primarily relied on each other for support. Day in and day out, year in and year out, we worked at keeping our love alive. We developed our own family traditions. We did our best to live our wedding vows: *for better or for worse until death us do part.*

My job that summer was still that of being a cheerleader for Dee as he again toiled on the streets of Pasadena, spending his days breaking up old concrete with a jack hammer, digging ditches, or pouring cement for curbs and gutters. Each evening he'd come home filthy dirty, every muscle sore, and dead tired. For a while he'd sit on the small concrete stoop outside the back door leading into the kitchen, then pull off his heavy boots, go inside and take a shower. I'd have some dinner ready by the time he'd cleaned up, and next one of two things would happen: either he would drive to Cal State LA to take one of the classes necessary for his California elementary teaching credential, or, shortly after dinner, he'd be in bed, sore and dead to the world. By the end of August, when he'd worked into better physical shape, it was time to put on a white shirt, tie and jacket and begin a new career as an eighth grade teacher at Washington School.

I was a full-time mom, but early in the summer I tried my hand at caring for two young children in our home. With two little ones of my own, I very shortly found I didn't have the patience to look after two more little ones, and I quit that effort in a hurry. If I remember rightly, one afternoon, not long after I had taken on the job, I walked my two little charges home to their mother, profusely apologizing, "I'm sorry, I just can't do this anymore." Serious fatigue is a very real 'burn out' for mothers of young children.

My next effort at supplementing our income was more satisfying. I became a reader of essays for an English teacher at Pasadena High School. I could read and correct the papers while the boys were napping or after they were down for the night. I liked that job. I liked being associated with education.

There's no mistaking it. I've always loved school. I love being connected with some kind of learning, whether I'm the student or I'm the teacher. I love being on either side of that equation. In that first fall living in Pasadena, I learned about adult education classes being offered through Pasadena City College, and I enrolled in an evening tailoring class. It was a good chance for a break from the little ones, and during the year I made a sport coat for my husband and sewed little red vests for our boys at Christmas.

More than the tailoring class, what really excited me that fall, also school-related, occurred the first day I took my two-year-old son to a parent education class, another adult education class also offered under the auspices of PCC. It was held at Hamilton School, only a block away, the same elementary school my husband had attended as a child.

One of my sister-in-law's neighbors, Marge Burns, who became a long-time friend and who also had two boys the same ages as ours, had told me about the program. She described how the parent was the student who observed and kept notes on her child and other children playing in a nursery school setting for part of the morning. Later, the mothers would sit with a teacher and talk about raising children. As I sat in the circle of parents that very first morning and looked out at the children playing, I said to myself, *This is what I want to do. This is what I want to teach.*

The first year I took Leon to Parent Ed (as it is still called), I brought Larry with us in a stroller, where he sat or slept while Leon played with the other children. Many other young mothers in my neighborhood were also in the group, and this helped me feel settled in my new home.

My husband enjoyed being a teacher, but feeling we could use the extra income, in the spring when Little League started up, he got a job with the San Gabriel Recreation Department. As soon as school was over for the day, he would change from his school clothes into a pair of jeans, T-shirt and sneakers, then go down to the Little League fields to prepare the baseball diamonds for the evening's games. He would rake the area, chalk the baselines, and put the bases on their corners before each game, repeating the process for the second game of the night. It would be almost nine o'clock before he got home. He worked hard to support his growing family.

The little two bedroom house had seemed quite comfortable for us when we moved in, but as the boys grew, we began thinking we needed a little more room. We also wanted a house which was a little farther distant from the noisy Del Mar Boulevard, just one house away. We began to think about moving. We hadn't gotten to the point of contacting a realtor when, one way or another, we discovered someone else on our street was also thinking about moving. Mrs. Blanche Haire, an older neighbor, who lived at 290 South Grand Oaks, just down the street, was planning to move closer to her son. Hers was an English Tudor-style, shingle house, a little larger than ours with three bedrooms and an attic, which, we imagined, could be converted into additional living space later on.

Mrs. Haire was ready to sell her house. We were ready to buy it. Call it serendipity, call it karma, call it whatever else you choose to describe these coincidences, but it was our good fortune. There was no agent and no commission to be paid. It was a win-win situation. We were able to get a loan and within ninety days we had moved in.

Between 1959 and 1974

There probably aren't many families who balance their belongings on their kids' wagon and pull it five houses down the street, but that's just what we did. I'm sure we must have begged, borrowed or hired a truck to move our major appliances. All I remember is our making innumerable trips up and down the block transferring dressers and boxes from one house to the other.

Ninety days had seemed like to us a long time to wait, but Mrs. Haire was nice enough to let me come down and plant some gladiola bulbs among the iris that colored her backyard. I planned for the gladiolas to be in full bloom when the house became our own. Each time I came I would thin out a few of the iris to make room for the new flowers. I wasn't disappointed.

The bright yellows and reds of the gladiolas, against a dark green hedge, were blooming profusely, when we finally moved in. But, one day, shortly after we had settled in, our son Leon came in from outside and proudly announced he had helped me weed the garden. I went outside, and there, to my horror, were all my beautiful new flowers decapitated, lying sadly on the ground. After all my hard work. I was devastated, but what could I do? He was just trying to help, doing what he had seen me do: cutting the tops off some of the flowers. Although terribly disappointed that my yard wouldn't make the pages of *Better Homes and Gardens,* I got over it, and we planted more.

We enjoyed the extra space in our new home. The boys still shared a bedroom, and the third bedroom, situated at the back of the house, we designated as a family room where we watched television, and where the children could be happy playing if we were having company.

Each week, until he was four, I took Leon to Hamilton School for our play-day at Parent Ed. In September, after his fourth birthday, I carpooled with three other mothers to another Parent Ed site, at San Raphael Elementary School, for a "Special Four" day. Younger children weren't allowed in this class so Larry stayed at home with Mrs. Julie Dutro, our beloved baby-sitter (we didn't call baby-sitters '*care-givers*' in those years). The next fall, with Leon in kindergarten, Larry and I walked over to Hamilton every Thursday morning, giving him the same nursery school experience while I observed, visited with other young mothers, and participated in the discussion group.

Although I had been prepared to teach at the secondary level, being in the Parent Ed setting captured my imagination. It would also be a perfect job for me, I thought, because it would always be only on a part-time basis. I could work a little and still be at home with the children. With both boys going to be in school (at least part-time for our kindergartner, Larry) in the fall, I felt the time was right to begin working. I expressed my interest in wanting to become a teacher in the program to one of my teachers. She relayed my message to the supervisor of the program, Dorothee Hodges, who, after checking into my qualifications, invited me to participate in the necessary 'cadet training,' the program's label for what was essentially 'practice teaching'. However, I would also have to take one or two classes to qualify for a California adult education credential with a specialization in early childhood education. Pacific Oaks College, located in Pasadena, which combined a nursery school with college classes in early childhood education, was a match for my needs. It was ideal. And best of all, I was going to be a student again.

I was thrilled to be accepted, and made plans for Mrs. Dutro, to watch Larry, and pick up Leon from kindergarten, while I went to school and participated in the cadet training program. I thrived on being in the role of a teacher, and at the end of the six weeks' period was offered an assignment for the fall.

That assignment had to be held in limbo, however, because I was pregnant again, expecting in late September. I couldn't accept the offer. Fortunately for me, the staff felt that I had the potential to be a good teacher, and Mrs. Hodges told me to give her a call when I was ready to join the staff.

* * * * *

Almost as soon as I realized I was pregnant, we had asked ourselves, "Where will the baby sleep?" We put the TV back into the living room, gave the boys the back bedroom, and, for the first time in our married lives, were able to plan a nursery for our baby-to-be. Because we didn't know whether it would be a boy or a girl (sonograms weren't routinely administered in 1961), we chose yellow and white as a color scheme and converted the smaller bedroom into a nursery.

Of course, I thought it would be especially nice to have a girl since we already had two boys, but my sister, Sharon, had had a girl in July, and my friend Joan Helble had also had a girl earlier in the year. I wasn't sure I'd be so lucky.

Unlike Larry's unexpected and early appearance, there was no drama when our daughter was born. When I was almost two weeks overdue, and in the doctor's office to be checked that Monday morning, our obstetrician, Dr. Tjaart Nanninga, said, "I think it's time. Why don't we just set this thing in motion?" After his office staff coordinated his schedule with that of the hospital we settled on the next day, October third. We arranged for Leon to be picked up by neighbors and driven to St. Philip's school where he was now a second grader, and for Mrs. Dutro to come before we left the house to walk Larry to kindergarten at Hamilton. I got up early and went to morning Mass at St. Philip's, and afterwards Dee and I drove up to St. Luke's Hospital where our baby was to be delivered.

As things were moving along in the labor room, Dr. Nanninga said to me, "Oh, did I tell you it's a girl?" No, he hadn't told us. I guess we hadn't asked. Still, I did not want to get my hopes up; I didn't want to be disappointed.

Once the baby had made her way into the world, the doctor held her up for us to see. I remember saying, almost in disbelief, "It *is* a girl. It *is* a girl." And a beautiful little girl she was, all eight pounds, two ounces of her. Or was it eight pounds, nine ounces? It's not important. What's important is I thought this was the most beautiful little girl ever to have been born. I'm sure her father thought the same thing.

We named our daughter Mary Catherine, and intended her to be called by both names: Mary Catherine. That, I must confess, was mostly my doing. I chose the name Mary for two reasons. The first reason was to honor Mary, Jesus' mother, and whom I wanted remembered each time my daughter's name was said. A second reason was because the name Mary is also akin to Mae, Dee's mother's middle name, Bertha Mae, as well as the middle name of my maternal grandmother, Ella Mae Ladd. The 'Catherine' of her name was chosen to honor my mother. In my mind's eye I could see a future engagement announcement in the Star-News, "Mr. and Mrs. Leon Crabb announce the engagement of their daughter, Mary Catherine to ?" whomever the lucky young man might be. It sounded so right. The full 'Mary Catherine' designation lasted only until she got into kindergarten and then, somehow, the 'Catherine' got left off and she became just 'Mary.' Occasionally a relative whom I don't see very often will still ask about 'Mary Catherine.'

Mary Catherine was an easy-going baby and by the spring semester of 1962, and knowing we would have our dear Mrs. Dutro as a baby-sitter, I felt ready to take on part-time teaching. I called the Parent Education office, and Mrs. Hodges assigned me two classes, each of which met one day a week. Almost eight years after graduating from college, I was going to have a real job.

Parent Ed classes were held in various locations throughout the Pasadena district: in schools, churches and parks. My first assignment was at Grant Park, located a short block from Cal Tech, the California Institute of Technology. Many of the mothers bringing their preschoolers to this group were wives of graduate students at Cal Tech. They provided an interesting mix of cultures and, being in an academic milieu, were all very anxious that their children be prepared for school and formal learning. It was both exciting and challenging. One of my favorite topics of discussion was one on traditions. Such an international group made for a wonderfully stimulating morning for both the teachers and the mothers.

However, I sometimes became frustrated because many of these mothers seemed not to enjoy their children at this age. Their anxiety over preparing the child for formal learning, deprived them of the innocence and joys of these preschool years, which, although parents don't realize it at the time, last such a short time.

One such mother, whose husband was a scientist at Cal Tech, and whose only child was not yet three, came to me during one of our classes and asked me, "What can I do for Brian?"

I knew she meant, "How can I prepare him for the skills of reading and printing?"

I went home that afternoon, and sat at our dining room table, pen in hand, trying to think of all the ways I could encourage her. I wanted to give her something to broaden both her and Brian's horizons. As my thoughts evolved, they crystallized into something more than just a to-do list. I wanted to talk about the intangible gifts parents have to offer, as well as the tangible skills children need.

"A Parent's Gift"

Gold and silver have I none,
What gift then can I give my son?

I can endow him with a sense of worth.
  I can deepen his inner security by developing self-esteem.
  I can encourage natural talents and special qualities.
  I can show an understanding of other cultures and other peoples

I can stimulate his sense of adventure.
  I can present to him a wide variety of experiences.
  I can feed his natural curiosity.
  I can help him develop an awareness of all life around him.

I can enrich his vocabulary.
  I can talk with him of many things, as opposed to talking "at" him.
  I can listen to him and welcome him unique expression of ideas.
  I can read to him from fact and fancy, poetry and prose.
  I can sing with him, old songs and new.

I can ignite the spark of his creativity.
  I can kindle his imagination.
  I can accept his new ideas.
  I can appreciate his efforts.
  I can provide him with the raw materials with which
    to work.
  I can give him time to dream.

I can mold his character.
  I can set a worthy example for him to follow.
  I can motivate him toward achieving honest goals.
  I can be reverent and hold certain values sacred.
  I can laugh with him when life tests us both.
  I can offer him love.

I taught in the Parent Education program, in Pasadena and the surrounding cities which comprise the Pasadena Community College District, for fourteen years, and have always felt it was in this setting I received the greatest satisfaction, and hoped I might been helpful to those many parents and children in my classes.

* * * * *

Following their kindergarten year at Hamilton Elementary School, Leon and I enrolled our sons at St. Philip's parochial school on Hill Street where we went to church. I wanted them to have a good foundation in both academics and knowledge of their Catholic religion. Both boys sang in the children's choir, and each became an altar server.

We also felt there were additional benefits and opportunities offered through the Pasadena public school system, and after each of the boys completed the sixth grade, we transferred them to Wilson Junior High (where Dee had gone to school) for two more years, and from Wilson they went on to Blair High School.

166

Leon played basketball at Blair, took four years of Latin and went to Rome with the Latin Club one spring break.

Larry chose to be in the band, where he played several instruments, and was awarded "Best Musician of the Year" in his senior year. The bandleader announced that his reason for choosing Larry was because whenever he needed a musician to fill in on one particular instrument, Larry would quickly learn to play it.

Mary, whom we had transferred from St. Philip's to Assumption of the Blessed Virgin Mary School after the first grade, was happy in her environment, and we were happy as well.

Over the years both boys took piano lessons from a Mrs. Brown and later Marlene Puccinelli; they played Little League and Babe Ruth baseball; they belonged to the Boy Scouts and enjoyed overnights and camp-outs, especially in the summer when they got to spend time at Camp Cherry Valley on Catalina Island. To earn spending money they mowed neighborhood lawns until they were old enough to get jobs as box boys at the grocery store a few blocks away. Larry also had a paper route. (Side note: Larry's paper route began on his birthday, the morning of the big Sylmar earthquake in 1971. As he saw transformers swaying back and forth emitting electrical currents, and felt the sidewalk beneath him undulate, he thought the world was coming to an end and got home as fast as he could pedal.)

Mary became a Girl Scout and I was her troop's leader along with two other mothers, Pat Greutert and Mary Shaw. We had some good times. We were also lucky enough to have Erwin Ward, the father of one of the girls, and who worked for the Forestry Service, give his time as a leader on hikes and campouts. Mary got to spend time during several summers at the Girl Scout camp at

White's Landing on Catalina Island. At the end of their eighth grade year, I and several other mothers took the troop on the ferry to Catalina where we camped at the isthmus of the island. Fortunately, or unfortunately, depending upon one's point of view, we were camped right next to a troop of Boy Scouts. Several of the girls were already interested in boys, and they really enjoyed that aspect of the trip. I think it was then and there I made up my mind to let someone else guide the troop through the teenage years.

Another of my scouting memories was the time, while camping up in the Azusa Canyon area, when some of the girls found a small dead rattlesnake and thought it would be fun to put it in my sleeping bag. I don't think they realized that the fangs still contained the snake's venom. Luckily, I found it before I crawled in for the night.

* * * * *

In 1958, shortly after we had moved back to Pasadena, Dee had come across an ad in the Star-News one Sunday morning: "Wanted: Banjo player for a Dixieland jazz band." I encouraged him to call the number listed. Although he had played the banjo ever since he was sixteen, had played with Bob McDonald and Jim Blanton at Idaho State, and whenever other opportunities presented themselves to strum that instrument, Dee had never played in a band before. The leader took him on. He became the banjo player in a newly organized band which was first called The Sad Sack Seven, and later dubbed The Southland Seven. Playing gigs, was a new dimension and another thread woven into the fabric of our married life. This aspect of our lives would last until a year before his death in 2003.

* * * * *

A few years after Leon and I had moved to Pasadena in 1956, my mother, father, brother and younger sisters had also moved to California. (Sharon lived there only one summer before she returned to college in Spokane, later married, and still lives there.) Dad hadn't been able to make a living on the farm in Careywood, and with young children to support, he needed a reliable income. He did not want to keep working in the mines, and for a year, the family lived in Redding, where Dad worked for his brother, CJ, in CJ's furniture store. Somehow I could never picture my dad being a salesman, and perhaps neither did he as the following year they moved to Seneca, in Plumas County, about a two-hour drive south and east of Redding, where my father was again employed to work at the only occupation in which he felt successful: mining. Again, he went to work underground. As my sister, Chris, wrote in her book, *Ten Days to Say Goodbye*, "Somehow, Dad connected with this man who owned a large lumber mill in Marysville and felt that there must still be gold in the mines that were opened during the gold rush. He hired Dad to bring a mine in Seneca up to safety standards so that they would be able to hire a crew and start mining." (p 19)

Every summer, our family would pile into the 1956 blue and white Plymouth station wagon we acquired

169

when the apple-green Plymouth we bought before leaving Pocatello seemed too small for our growing family. We'd drive north to visit Mom and Dad, and my brother and sisters in Seneca for a week or so. On the way we would stop in Stockton to visit our friends from Idaho State, the McDonald's, where Dee and Bob would hammer out their music on the piano and banjo, and we'd recall those drinking songs we'd sung so many times years before.

It was an adventure going to Seneca, located five miles down a dirt road stemming off from the main highway at Canyondam, which itself was just a wide spot in the road, with only a post office, bar, and gas station. The closest town to Canyondam was Greenville, eleven or so miles to the southeast. Seneca had been a thriving community in the early days of the California gold rush. Now a ghost town, an old wooden building still stood with a sign painted in the window which read: GOLD DUST EXCHANGED HERE.

Mother and Dad, Chris and Terry, and Don (before he went away to college and then into the army) lived in an old two-story house with no electricity. It wasn't as primitive as it might sound. The stove and refrigerator were fueled by propane gas, and they had indoor plumbing. As it became dark, the house was lit with kerosene lamps. Television was the only modern advantage they lacked. In the evenings, after dinner and dishes were done, Mom and Dad would sit and read while the kids did their homework, or they'd play cards or board games. In the summertime, Dad would go down to a little bar called "The Gin Mill," drink and play horseshoes. He took Dee down there a few times when we visited. Mother and I never went.

Because my sister Terry was just a few months younger than our son Leon, and Chris was only five years older, our boys had a wonderful time playing with their aunts, climbing up the mountain side, going down the "goat trail" and wading in the Feather River that flowed downstream just across the road from our house. My dad enjoyed teaching his 'city' son-in-law how to fly fish. The biggest catch Dee made was one afternoon when he hooked a fly into his own eyebrow. Thank God it wasn't an inch lower.

Most nights, when we visited, after we got the kids to bed, Mom and I would partner against Dee and Dad in a game of bridge. It made Mom so mad when they won almost every time. "They don't even know how to bid," she'd say. "They just play by the seat of their pants."

One year when we had driven up to spend Thanksgiving at Seneca, just before we left for Pasadena, Dad went out into the woods and found a beautiful silver-tip pine tree, which we tied to the top of our station wagon and kept standing in a bucket of water in our garage in Pasadena until it was time to bring it into the house to decorate as our Christmas tree. It looked and smelled as fresh as the day it had been cut down. Another year, Dad sent us a box of five small silver-tips, graduated in size. We decorated three for the bay window of the living room and the children had the other two in their bedrooms.

I'm not sure, when we visited that summer, whether Mother told me that my dad's health was failing, or if I realized, when I saw him during our time there he did not look at all well, but, in 1963, Leon and I made the decision to drive up to Seneca the day after Christmas to spend the rest of our vacation with my family. As usual, we had a good time. Both of our boys, in later years, told me, without knowing what the other had said, that as we were getting ready to leave Seneca on our last day, their granddad slipped a silver dollar into the palm of each boy's hand as he shook their hands to say goodbye. It is one of their fondest memories.

As we pulled away up the dusty road, I looked back and waved to my family who stood in the yard, watching us leave. As fate would have it, this was the last time I saw my father alive. Shortly afterwards, his doctor discovered Paul had tuberculosis. (Or perhaps my parents already knew and didn't tell me.) Mother drove him down to the Weimar Medical Center, then a sanitarium for TB patients, located in the Sierra Nevada foothills, about 40 miles north of Sacramento. There, on April 2, 1964, my father had a heart attack and died, alone and without his family surrounding him, without a loved one to hold his hand.

I got the telephone call later that day. My brother, Don, serving in the army, was stationed in Germany at the time, but, through the Red Cross, Mother got the sad message to him. Within a few days he was able to fly back to California. As soon as I could arrange for someone to take my classes, I made plans to go to Seneca for the funeral. Because Mary Catherine was not yet three years old, and it would have been a hardship for us to have someone carrying for her while I was gone, I took her with me on the Greyhound bus. My sister Sharon wasn't able to come from Spokane where she was living; she was several months pregnant and had three

172

other children at home. Mother was at the bus station to meet me when we arrived in Greenville.

I remember going with her to the funeral home, and seeing Daddy's body lying in an open casket. Instinctively I reached over and touched his arm, saying, "Oh, Daddy, we loved you so much." To this day I remember that moment. When I touched his body it was very cold. I might even have gasped. I don't know what I had expected, but I don't believe, in all my sheltered life, I'd ever seen a dead body before, let alone touched one. Those were my last words to him. "Oh, Daddy, we loved you so much."

When my brother, Don, arrived home, he and I met with the Methodist minister in Greenville, and we arranged the details of the funeral service. Mother said she just couldn't do it. As we talked about what we might like to have included, I chose the scripture passage from John 14:2 in the King James Version of the Bible that reads, "In my Father's house are many mansions: if it were not so, I would have told you. I go to prepare a place for you." In my heart I felt that my own father was a very good, hard-working man who loved his family, and there would definitely be room in a mansion for him in heaven.

Following Dad's funeral in Greenville, the owner of the bar and restaurant on the highway at Canyondam, just at the junction where the dirt road descended into the canyon to Seneca, invited everyone at the funeral to come and celebrate Paul's life. It seemed a little strange to me, maybe even a little irreverent, to be celebrating in a bar, but on the other hand it was not so strange: Dad spent a lot of his life enjoying the camaraderie of friends in bars. He'd be very much at home here.

Without Paul, there was no reason for my mother to stay in California. Don was in the army and not living at home, so as soon as the school year was over for my younger sisters, who were then nine and thirteen, Mother, who was only fifty-three years old, moved back to Kellogg to be near her mother. Because of the distance from Pasadena to northern Idaho, and our kids being involved in their own summer activities, visits with my mom and the younger girls were much less regular after 1964.

* * * * *

In the summer of 1965, Leon and I and our three kids made an extended road trip across the country, taking six weeks to drive from "sea to shining sea," in our blue and white Plymouth station wagon, camping most of the way, sleeping in a big blue three-room tent that we had purchased from a Sears catalog. We visited Leon's relatives in Kansas and New Mexico. My friend, Joan, and her husband, John, were stationed in Virginia at the time, and we stayed with them for a few days. We saw Lincoln's tomb in Illinois, drove through New York City, saw the Statue of Liberty, and spent a day or two in Washington, DC. I had written our congressman and Senator George Murphy requesting tours of several government buildings. Leon, who was teaching American history to eighth graders at the time, made it a living history lesson for the family. That trip is a story in itself, one that will have to wait for another telling. Our Super 8 movie camera helped us recall some of the highlights of over three thousand miles of adventure.

* * * * *

Filled with the success of this trip I talked Leon into considering the possibility of driving the Alcan Highway to Alaska in the near future, and began planning. That adventure might have become a reality had not our single car, shingled garage burned down the next summer with the big blue tent and all our camping gear stored in it. I lost my heart for the adventure, thinking of everything we'd have to replace. We never took our kids to Alaska.

The garage fire happened on a hot Tuesday afternoon in July. I was in the house when our next-door neighbor telephoned. "There's smoke coming from your backyard." I ran to the kitchen window, saw the flames, and immediately called the fire department. By the time they got there, only a few minutes later, they weren't able to save much more than the shell of the structure.

Later that afternoon I telephoned Leon, who was staying in Sacramento for two weeks, attending a National Science Foundation workshop for which he'd received a grant. I gave him the bad news. "You've got to come home," I bawled into the phone. "The garage burned down."

After asking a few questions he said, "I can't come home until the weekend. We cover too much material every day. I'll have to drop out if I miss the next three days. I'll be home as early as I can on Friday night." I cried some more.

Somehow, I made it through the next three days, and Leon made a quick turn-around trip home over the weekend. The fire department listed the cause of the fire as spontaneous combustion: oily rags on a hot, hot day, lying on a workbench below the shard of a broken window.

Leon came home at the end of his workshop, and over the next few weeks we did the usual tasks that go along with an insurance company's requirements before adjudicating monies to replace the garage. We made an inventory of its contents, refreshing our memories by thumbing through the pages of our trusty Sears catalog. "Oh, we had one of those," one of us would say, pointing to some tool or implement, "...and one of these, and two of those," and page after page would hold some memory for us. When we were satisfied that we'd recalled all that we had lost, we filed insurance claims and hired a carpenter to build us a new double garage. It was a very traumatic experience.

The following spring, as I was rounding the corner onto our street one Saturday morning, shortly before noon, bringing Mary back from a Girl Scout outing, I spied a red fire truck parked in the proximity of our house. My heart leapt into my throat. Oh, no! It couldn't be us—again. But it was. I parked the car across the street and ran across the lawn to where my husband was standing.

Leon had been preparing to repaint the house, using a small propane torch to soften the old dry paint which he would then scrape away. He had just finished the front section he was working on, had put the torch away, and was examining his work when he heard a crackling sound between the shingles and the inner wall by the front bay window. Smoke began seeping through the tinder dry shingles. Quickly he grabbed a garden hose lying in the yard and stuck it into the area, but this wasn't enough to quench the fire. He ran inside and called the fire department. By the time they arrived the flames had spread and reached the roof.

When time is of the essence, what do you try to save? In our case, Leon grabbed his banjo first. Neighbors helped haul out small chairs. I looked for our photo albums. Thanks to the quick-acting firemen who covered our living room with tarps, we lost only the front part of the house, and no possessions that couldn't be replaced.

There was also a bright side to the accident. Because we needed a new roof, we decided to add two bedrooms and a full bath in the attic. Leon and Larry shared the larger bedroom, and Mary had a smaller bedroom. The boys' former bedroom became a comfortable family room, and the nursery became a small office. When the garage had burned down the year before, another friend, a landscape architect, had offered to design a new backyard setting for us, so we now had a very comfortable environment to call home. It was just right for our growing family.

* * * * *

During our fifteen years at 290 SGO, we created many other, more pleasant, memories. For weeks one summer, in our backyard, all the neighborhood children rehearsed a play, "Rip Van Winkle," and gave a splendid performance for all the parents and neighbors. Every year the Crabbs and Campbells shared BBQs and Fourth of July celebrations. (In northern California, to this day, now into the fifth generation, descendants of our two families continue our Fourth of July tradition.)

I'd say we were just your average American family, three children and three pets--a little Beagle named Candy, and two black cats, Jinx and Stitch. And we were very blessed: each of us was healthy; we lived in a comfortable home we could afford; and Leon had a job that paid all the bills. Did we know and appreciate it at the time? I'm not sure. We were busy pursuing our dreams: going on to school, thinking of better jobs, raising the children, taking vacations, having some fun.

I was working part-time as a Parent Ed teacher in Pasadena and the surrounding communities, but knew no full-time teachers were ever hired in this program. Realizing I would eventually like to teach full-time, I also kept going to school. By enrolling in Pasadena College, a four-year Nazarene college with a campus only a mile or so from where we lived, I earned my California elementary teaching credential.

Leon had set his sights on becoming a school principal. He was enrolled at Whittier College and began

177

taking courses leading toward a master's degree and an administrative credential. By going to evening classes and summer sessions, within three years he had completed the program and let it be known in the district he would apply for a principal's position when an opening occurred.

He was not hired to fill the first vacancy that came up in the district. However, in 1968, when Mr. Cokeley, one of the principals who had been on Leon's hiring committee, retired from Washington School, Leon was appointed to replace him. He was to be the principal of the school where he had begun his teaching career eleven years earlier. With that position came another broadening of our horizons. We began socializing with the other administrators in the district; Leon got to go to conferences and conventions and sometimes I went with him. He joined the local Kiwanis club and our circle of friends widened further.

* * * * *

For our fifteenth wedding anniversary, in 1968, we decided to celebrate by spending the weekend on Catalina Island, located twenty-six miles off the coast of California. Leon had been there many years earlier with his friend, Rod Jennings. Mrs. Dutro agreed to stay with the children and we got all gussied up for the trip. I remember wearing a pleated white skirt with a pink floral top and white summer heels. Leon may or may not have worn a tie, but he was dressed in nice casual slacks and sport coat, shiny shoes. We packed our overnight bag and drove down to a hangar in Long Beach from where we were to take off in a small plane. As we approached the plane we looked at the five or six other passengers who were going along with us. They were all attired in shorts, Hawaiian shirts and flip-flops. We felt totally out of place. Like real rubes. That evening as we were strolling along the bayside on Crescent Avenue, we could see and hear the boat owners lounging on decks, having drinks, and laughing with their friends. From one boat we heard a cornet player blowing the notes of "Birth of the Blues." It seemed to us the boat owners were having much more fun on the water than we were on the shore.

Leon told one of the teachers at Washington School, Gen Petrey, about our weekend, and soon afterwards she and her husband, Harry, invited us to go out with them on their sailboat. When Harry invited Leon to crew with him on a weekend race, Leon really got the sailing bug. We took Power Squadron courses, learned the terminology and the basics of sailing, and joined the Pasadena Power Squadron. We also soon bought our first sail boat, the *Genesis*, a Cal 20 with the registration number 1515. (I'm looking at a small model of it, even as I write, and it brings back such warm memories.) We moored it at a dock in a private marina in Los Alamitos Bay, an hour's drive from Pasadena.

Lady V (renamed *Sweet Lady*)

That summer, with the knowledge that we had other boats, which could come to our rescue if we got in trouble, we joined a flotilla of others in the Power Squadron and cruised to Catalina Island. Sailing to Catalina Island was great adventure. We always saw some kind of sea life along the way, mostly dolphins, jelly fish, even flying fish on occasion. On rocks close to the island we could sometimes see elephant seals. Larry often sat in the stern of the boat with a fishing rod trailing and bobbing along our wake. Once in a while he would catch a fish, bonito or barracuda. One summer, in the *Genesis*, we circumnavigated the island, taking a week sailing from harbor to harbor. Another time, with our friends Al and Doloris Williams, we sailed as far as San Diego and back.

* * * * *

Our circle of friends had widened, our financial circumstances had improved, but we were still living on the same street that my husband had lived on from the time he was in kindergarten. By 1974, our son Leon had graduated from high school and was off to college at San Diego State; his brother Larry would be a senior at Blair High School, and, when she was ready, we were planning to send Mary to Alverno Academy, a Catholic girls' high school in the northeast area of Pasadena. It seemed a good time to make a change. We began looking for a newer house in a newer neighborhood. We even looked at some new condominiums that were going up just a few blocks away. We asked if they sold to families with children. "You can have boys who are sixteen or older, but any girls have to be at least eighteen." (Such restrictions would be illegal in this day and age.) When we asked why the owners made that the distinction, the answer came back, "Because boys spend their time at their girlfriends' homes, and girls bring their boyfriends home. It sometimes causes problems."

We wanted a home where Mary would want to bring her friends. Wouldn't it be nice if that house had a swimming pool? We began looking at For Sale signs on houses in the Upper Hastings Ranch development of Pasadena. Within two blocks of Alverno Academy we found just what we were looking for at 3810 Edgeview Drive. We even liked the sound of the address.

Edgeview Drive, located near the top of Upper Hastings, lies just four blocks from the base of the San Gabriel Mountain foothills. Only one block long, the street runs east and west. The house at 3810 is situated on the south side of the street, with a view that extends as far as the Pacific Ocean on a clear day. In the distance we could see the flight path of planes flying into LAX, and occasionally we could see Catalina Island.

The one-story stucco house was designed with sliding glass doors which opened from the living room and two of the bedrooms onto the small yard with a good-sized swimming pool with a slide descending from one end of it into the water. The kids thought the slide was great. We made an offer, and in April, 1974, we moved to our new home.

Between 1974 and 1999

The time had arrived for me to seriously look for full-time employment, a job with benefits, a position that might hold the potential for broadening my scope of responsibility. I had finished all the work I needed for a California elementary teachers credential and had contacted the Pasadena Unified School District, and more than ten other school districts within a comfortable driving distance, inquiring about possible openings for teachers. Although I had been teaching Parent Ed classes for fourteen years, I was without any actual elementary or secondary classroom teaching experience beyond student teaching. Despite all my applications, I received only one interview, and that one did not result in the offer of a contract.

Next, I pursued possible openings in the local parochial schools. Luckily, Assumption of the Blessed Virgin Mary School, which our daughter attended, had an opening for a fourth grade teacher. I applied and was hired for the 1974-75 school year. It was great that Mary and I got to ride to and from school together each day. I was co-leader of the Girl Scout troop at the school, and we worshipped as a family every Sunday at the church.

Although I'd been teaching Parent Ed for many years, having thirty-eight students in a classroom all day long was a horse of a different color, and sometimes I thought that horse was going to buck me out of the saddle. But I learned, along with the students, and was happy with my decision to make the move. Things were going smoothly until one spring afternoon.

I was having a parent conference in my classroom after school had been dismissed for the day. Mary, now in the eighth grade, was biding her time in the schoolyard, waiting for me to take her home. When she saw a man, whom she didn't recognize, walking into the playground, she felt uneasy, walked quickly down to the girls' bathroom and went inside. Very soon, the door opened and the man she had seen peered in. She remembers glancing into the mirror and thinking he must have misread the sign on the door, presuming it was the boys' bathroom. The door closed, but a moment

182

later it reopened, the man walked inside, and grabbed her from behind, holding a sharp object to her neck.

"Don't scream or I'll kill you," he said.

Holding her near to him, they walked out of the bathroom, past my closed classroom door, which had a small window in the upper portion. *Maybe Mom will see me,* Mary remembers thinking to herself. I hadn't looked up. A second chance for them to be seen by me also went for naught. The kidnapper's car was parked on Orange Grove in an area clearly visible from the front windows of my classroom, but, involved in discussing my student's progress with his mother, I did not look up to see Mary and her abductor get into his car and drive away.

However, on their way to the car, Mary's sweater dropped to the sidewalk.

When my parent conference was over, I said goodbye to the parent, thanked her for coming, and walked outside, ready to go home. There was no Mary in sight. I looked around the school yard. No Mary. I walked inside and around the church. No Mary. I walked out onto the sidewalk bordering Orange Grove. No Mary. But I did recognize the sweater I saw on the sidewalk. It belonged to Mary.

My heart began to thump in my chest and a lump formed in my throat. It was not like her to leave the school yard without telling me. I ran into the school office, asked to use the telephone and called home. No answer. I called a couple of her friends to see if she'd walked home with them. No luck.

I called Leon at school. "Mary's gone," I remember saying. "I can't find her."

"I'll be right home," he said.

After hanging up I went back into the church and prayed. I prayed especially to Mary, Jesus' mother, and after whom our daughter was named. *Please let my Mary be safe,* I begged.

I went back to the school office and our pastor, Father Crean, who had been informed by the office secretary Mary was nowhere to be found, called the police. With nothing more to be done at school, I drove home to see if she was there. No Mary.

I don't recall how long I had been at home before the phone rang. It was Father Crean calling to tell me Mary was with him in the rectory, and she was okay. I sped back to school, found her safe and unharmed. I called home again to leave a message for Leon that Mary was with me, she was all right, and we'd be home in just a few minutes.

Soon, the police arrived. In recalling the incident for the very kind policewoman who had come up to the school, Mary said the man had driven across town, and had parked in a school yard in the San Rafael area of Pasadena, on the other side of the Arroyo. The two talked. He said he went to church. Mary asked him where. "I can't tell you that," he replied. She said he told her he knew he was sick. Mary asked, "How can I help?"

"How can I help?" That is the only piece of her conversation with her kidnapper I remember Mary telling us about. I don't remember his response, but after a while, she said, he started his car, drove back in the direction of Assumption School, and stopped on Orange Grove Boulevard, about three blocks west of the school.

"Get out, count to fifty, don't turn around, and don't look up," he said. Mary opened the door, got out and stood on the sidewalk, counting to fifty. When she looked up, she didn't recognize any of the houses around her, wasn't sure just where she was, and was anxious to get off that street. "Just in case," she said "he might change his mind and drive back again looking for me."

She crossed the wide boulevard and walked north toward the mountains. Once she reached the next corner, Paloma Street, she recognized several familiar buildings, got her bearings, walked east to the next corner, and then back down toward Orange Grove where the school was now within sight. As soon as she turned into the driveway of the playground area she ran down to my classroom, but it was locked. She looked around for my car, and when she didn't see it she ran over to the nun's convent, whose backdoor opened onto the playground. One of the sisters let her inside, then called Father Crean, who, as soon as he hung up the phone, called me at home.

The rest of that fateful evening and night has faded in my memory. The next day her father and I drove down to the Pasadena police station with Mary, where she looked at photos of possible suspects. I'm not sure if she identified any of them as her kidnapper. As far as I know, the man was never apprehended.

After we left the police station, the three of us took a long drive, heading out of town, north on Highway 101. We drove as far as Camarillo, then returned home along the ocean, by way of Malibu and Santa Monica. We needed a change of scenery, if even for a short while.

I believe one other detail is relevant to this story. A week or so before this incident, I had invited a woman to come speak to the girls at our Girl Scout troop meeting about personal safety. I think her advice to remain calm in a dangerous situation is what might have helped save Mary's life, or at least prevented her from being raped. For that reason and, I also sincerely believe, that in answer to my prayers for Mary's intercession to protect my child, God spared our daughter.

We were spared. Once again we were blessed with the gift of our daughter.

Oh, yes, there's yet another addendum to this story. When our daughter became a mother with a daughter of her own, Mary did not seem to let this incident define how she reacted to her own daughter's safety. She was not overly protective. She shared her story with her children and they don't seem to have been traumatized by hearing it. I think I'm the one who remembers the incident with such anxiety. As I recall, the rest of the year at Assumption School continued without further trauma.

Shortly after the spring semester began, an envelope addressed to me arrived at our house. The return address read *Pasadena City College*. Inside was a flyer with a job description for a "Parent Education Specialist." The position would begin in mid-July. Hana Pearl Alexander, the current administrator of the program and my former boss, was retiring. I didn't know who mailed me the information, but took it as a sign that someone from the campus felt I might be a viable candidate. I read through the list of responsibilities, and felt, with my fourteen years of teaching in the program, I could qualify for the position.

I made an appointment with Hana Pearl (we never called her 'Mrs. Alexander'), and at the appointed time drove to PCC, walked into the 'C' Building, and down to her office. There were a number of questions I wanted to ask her, but more importantly, I sought her advice. She encouraged me to apply. However, there was one criterion which I did not meet: the position required that the applicant hold a master's degree in early childhood education, or be in the process of acquiring that degree.

If I wanted to be considered for the position, I'd need to get enrolled in a college or university *post haste*. Pasadena College, the Nazarene college where I had earned my teaching credential, had moved its campus to

Point Loma (and renamed it Nazarene University). Leon and I talked it over, and we made the decision I should apply to the University of LaVerne (then called LaVerne College), located about twenty-five miles east of Pasadena, and one which had the reputation of having a strong early childhood program. I immediately sent for all my transcripts, filled out an application, made an appointment, and drove out to meet with the appropriate personnel. My application was accepted, and once again I was a student. I was thrilled.

I also completed and submitted the application form for the position of Parent Education Specialist. From that day forward, I waited apprehensively for a letter or phone call that would tell me I'd been granted an interview. With Leon's guidance, I spent the next month preparing for "The Interview." We wrote out multiple questions and formulated answers I thought would put me in a good light with the interview panel. I also considered my appearance, and planned what I should wear to the interview. It had to be something appropriate, but not too severe nor too imposing. If I were selected to be among the finalists, there would be a second interview with the Vice-president for Instruction and I'd need something more formal for that occasion.

I went shopping and found a dark brown and white polka-dot sleeveless dress with a matching long-sleeved jacket. It fit perfectly. Then I waited... and waited... and waited... It seemed forever. Finally, the phone call came to arrange a time for an interview.

The first interview panel consisted of two current staff members, Mrs. Alexander, and the supervisor of the umbrella Adult Education-Continuing Education Department. We met in a small anteroom off the main office space on the lower floor of the 'C' Building.. I remember nothing of the interview except for the last question. "If you were to be considered for this position, would you be willing to come in for another interview?" I don't know what got into me, but I slapped the table with my hand and exuberantly replied, "You bet I would." They all laughed, and I chuckle whenever I think of the scene.

Luckily, I was invited back a second time. Somewhere I had read that you should dress for the job you want, so I bought another new outfit, one more suitable, I thought, for an administrator. This time the interview was held in the Vice-president's office with a different panel of teachers and administrators. I was asked a broader set of questions, ones more geared to determining my administrative capabilities and leadership ability. I must have answered to their liking because I was offered the position as Parent Education Specialist, an eleven-month assignment, to begin in the middle of July.

Now, I could really say that I had a 'career,' not just a job, but a 'career.' And I was back in school again, on my way to earning a master's degree. *How did the little girl from Idaho, the hard-rock miner's daughter, manage that? Have I always defined my life by referring to my Idaho roots? Somehow I seem to forget I was born in Los Angeles, California.*

* * * * *

Our world had already begun to expand. In the summer of 1974, Leon and I were invited by the PTA president at Washington School to join her and her two boys on a trip to visit her mother and grandmother in Landstuhl, Germany. Coming along with us were Leon's secretary, Kate Harris, her husband, John, and the Vice-principal, Ethyl Burton. We flew to London and spent a few days there before traveling on to Germany. From Landstuhl Maria took us on a road trip through other towns in Germany as well as Austria, and Lichtenstein. This was my first trip to Europe, and I came home feeling the experience had changed my life. It's been forty years since we took that trip, and I've seen many other parts of the world since then, but I still remember the awe I felt at my first sight of the magnificent castles and cathedrals, the food, the costumes and cultures, so different from our own. I came to the realization that the United States was only a small segment of the planet Earth.

My husband's world was also expanding on the home front. He was elected president of the Kiwanis Club in San Gabriel in 1975, and we both were able to go to the district and international conventions that year. The Kiwanis International Convention was held in Atlanta, Georgia. We were inspired by outstanding speakers and programs. The Cal-Nev-Ha District Convention took us to Honolulu, Hawaii. Not Los Angeles or Las Vegas, but Honolulu. How lucky was that as a 'two-for-one' trip?

What's a 'two for one' trip? It's one where one of us has our way paid, and the other gets to tag along. Many of our band trips were 'two-for-one's. (Band cruises were even better. We might have to pay for my air transportation, but once on the ship, we would have both our ways paid.) Traveling became one of our favorite pastimes.

We continued to enjoy sailing our Cal 20 on weekends around the Long Beach harbor. One evening we got a call from one of our friends in the marina. He told Leon, because of his health, he was going to have to sell his Catalina 27, and asked if we'd be interested in buying it. Of course we would. We had no trouble selling the *Genesis*, and now owned an even more seaworthy boat, re-named *Sweet Lady*, to sail over to Catalina Island.

Twice we sailed with two other couples and their boats for a long weekend at the island.

Each of the other couples had two children (teens, actually) the same ages as our Larry and Mary. The six kids had great fun rowing ashore in their dinghies, wandering through Avalon, and playing games in the Arcade. Our son, Leon, was living in San Diego at the time and he seldom sailed with us.

When a slip opening became available at the Dana Point Harbor marina, we sailed the *Sweet Lady* down to her new home and soon joined the Dana Point Yacht Club. We cruised with them to Catalina more than once. We even bought Mary a little sabot, and she learned to sail with the DPYC juniors.

Being at the DP Harbor was especially convenient for us because Leon's other love, his banjo-playing, had begun to take on a larger role in our lives. He was now a permanent member of the Golden Eagle Jazz Band which was drawing more and more fans as they played a gig every Sunday afternoon at the San Juan Capistrano Depot, only a ten-minute drive from the harbor. The band had also been invited to play at a few jazz festivals, and had been gaining a national reputation in that genre of music with a couple of CDs they had recorded.

Those were halcyon days. 'Halcyon' so aptly describes those times. The word was coined, my dictionary reads, after a bird formerly believed to have the power of calming wind and waves while it nested at sea. But halcyon days never last forever.

In 1981, Leon had a heart attack, and, for whatever reasons or fears, we never again sailed the *Sweet Lady* out of the harbor. We would sometimes drive down to Dana Point, sit out on her deck, reading or enjoying our drinks, and sleeping down below on a weekend when he was playing jazz at the San Juan Capistrano Depot. But my husband never again took her out of the slip. Eventually we sold a half-interest to his nephew, Gene

Crabb, and then, when it was obvious that our sailing days were over, we sold Gene the other half. As I say now, "It was a good gig while it lasted."

The boat had been a good place to go when the stress of our jobs as administrators almost got the best of us. Leon and I were able to support each other during those stressful periods when our workplace struggles seemed overwhelming. He had one superintendent who put so much pressure on him I swore to myself I'd go shoot the man if anything happened to my husband while he was on the job.

Then again, I also had one boss who made work so difficult for me I was advised by one of the administrators to take a stress-related leave of absence from the college. Only when our wonderful physician, Dr. Kathleen DeRemer, told me, in no uncertain terms, "You cannot let this woman make you think you're incompetent," and gave me reading material which boosted my spirits and offered advice for dealing with difficult situations, did I strengthened my resolve to return the next day, with renewed energy, to stay the course. I survived what might have been a crisis in my career.

One funny sidelight about our working days: While Mary was still living at home, she said she could always tell when Mom or Dad had had a bad day at work by the way they ate their dinner. She observed that if we'd had a bad day, we would sit at the kitchen table after dishing up our meal, put forks to our food, then the forks to our mouths, faster, faster, faster, shaking our heads sideways. Then forks back to the plates, forks to our mouths, forks to the plate, forks to the mouth, re-living some incident that we couldn't get out of our minds. Thankfully, we survived those moments and both of us made it to retirement age.

Both Leon and I continued our formal education almost to the year we each retired. He enrolled in an educational doctoral program at the University of LaVerne, while I enrolled in a Ph.D. program at Claremont Graduate School, now renamed Claremont Graduate University.

Leon's program took a very hands-on approach to educational leadership, and he enjoyed it immensely, completing all the prerequisite coursework leading up to his dissertation. At that point he decided that he would have to give up playing with the Golden Eagle Jazz Band if he were to take the time necessary to do research and write the dissertation. He didn't aspire to becoming a superintendent or even seeking another position with more responsibilities. He would rather make people happy playing his banjo with the Golden Eagle Jazz Band. For him to choose the band over the doctorate was a good decision. In his music lay his true passion.

Golden Eagle Jazz Band

Life with the Golden Eagle Jazz Band became a major part of our later lives. For twenty-two years, with few exceptions, Leon played banjo with the Golden Eagle Jazz Band at the Depot in San Juan Capistrano every Sunday afternoon. While he was gone I would work on my coursework, first on my master's degree, then later for my doctorate. It was a win-win situation.

My Life Defined...

We enjoyed our many travels to jazz festivals with the band. Besides various venues around the United States, including four cruises to Alaska and several cruises in the Caribbean, they played in Baja California, Scotland, Japan and Italy. We sometimes expanded our time on these gigs to take side-trips with our friends, Ken and Flossie Smith. Ken and Leon would often take their instruments out at a rest stop or a deserted stretch of the highway and get in a little rehearsal time. Leon reveled in the camaraderie of other musicians, especially banjo players. I might sum it up by saying, "Through education Leon made a living, through his music he made a life."

My responsibilities at PCC expanded over the years. From being in charge of only the Parent Education program, I became responsible for more areas of the non-credit adult education program, and eventually transferred to the credit side of the instruction division. Unlike Leon, whose love of his music caused him some ambivalence when he felt he had to choose one over the other, I felt no pull from another direction and was happy to keep pursuing my goal of earning a doctorate. In the college milieu there were many more possibilities for advancement if one had a Ph.D. appended to his or her name. I also had a less professional motive for pursuing my degree, one I probably shouldn't even have the nerve to admit. I had a vision of wearing, along with the traditional black cap, a black gown enhanced with three velvet stripes across the arms, as I marched with the faculty at commencement ceremonies each spring. These three stripes signified the wearer had earned a doctoral degree. I wanted to be one of them. Ah, vanity.

However, a few years into my studies, immediately following Leon's heart attack, I was forced to weigh the decision of whether or not to continue my program. Leon would need time to recuperate, and I would need to be there for him. I pondered my choices. I remember thinking, *If he dies, I'll be sorry I didn't finish. If he lives, I'll be sorry I didn't finish.* From that point on I kept my eye on the prize. Leon survived. I was there for him when he needed me, and I kept on with my classes.

When all my course work was completed, and it was time to work on my dissertation, I requested a sabbatical leave from the administration. I was told by the president of the college at the time, "We don't grant sabbaticals to administrators. Sabbaticals are only for faculty members." Although we knew it would be quite a challenge for us financially, with only one income for an entire school year, Leon and I arrived at the decision that I would ask to take a year of personal leave, without pay, for educational purposes.

The leave was granted, a temporary administrator was assigned to my position, and I began the research phase of the program. In retrospect, as well as allowing me time to finish my degree, other benefits also ensued, one of which I had not anticipated.

First, Leon and I learned we could live on only one salary. If he decided it was time for him to retire while I kept working, we would get along just fine. But, more importantly for me, this period of independence from my career while I was doing research and writing, helped me understand my personal identity, my self-image, was not dependent upon my administrative position or title at Pasadena City College. This was not an outcome to which I had previously given much thought. No thought at all, for that matter. But it definitely was a bonus, maybe even more important than my accomplishing the goal of earning a doctorate.

Pauline Crabb, Ph.D.

Also surprising to me, when I returned to the college campus the next fall with the new title of Dr. Crabb, was my amazement at how others' perception of who I was seemed to have changed. It was as if I were a different person from the one who had left the year before. Maybe I was. Who knows?

Leon retired in 1990, after 34 years in the San Gabriel School District. But his retirement from San Gabriel was not the end of his professional career as an educator. Within a short time he was recruited to be an interim principal in a neighboring school district. He also served in that same capacity in San Gabriel more than once. Additionally, he became an adjunct faculty member of Chapman University where he supervised student teachers fulfilling their practice teaching requirements in elementary schools in the area. He enjoyed that role, and was happy to say that he, as well as I, was a college faculty member.

I continued working at PCC until June, 1994, when I retired as the Assistant Dean of Instruction. There was no other dean to whom I reported; my immediate supervisor was Dr. David Ledbetter, Vice President for Instruction. My responsibilities lay in the area of curriculum development with each of the instructional departments. I was also responsible for coordinating the publication of the college catalog, and involved in staff development for the management team. Mine was an interesting career, and, despite a few bumps in the road (and who doesn't have them?), it was a very satisfying aspect of my life.

Within a month of my retirement, another adventure awaited us. That summer, the Golden Eagle Jazz Band was invited to play at the Edinburgh Jazz Festival. Leon and I, with no jobs calling us home in the middle of August, traveled to Scotland with the band. Prior to the festival we explored the countryside with Ken (cornet player in the GEJB) and Flossie Smith, our usual traveling companions on band trips. Then, for eleven days, we shared a rented flat in Edinburgh while the "boys" played their music at various festival venues. It was an exhilarating experience.

One afternoon outside a train station on Prince Street, a few of our band members, including Leon, were busking (translate: playing for small change), with the trombone player's honey-pot mute positioned out in front of the musicians to collect coins. I was there handing out to any interested passer-by fliers advertising the location of a gig where the band would be playing for the next few nights. I thought, *If only my boss at Pasadena City College could see me now.*

We had many other memorable band trips, with enough anecdotes to fill several books. Leon and I also took many other trips, independently of the band. We loved to travel and experience adventure.

* * * * *

As my siblings began to have families of their own, we tried to gather as a Crawford clan at least once every five years, with at least all of Mom's five children present, to celebrate our being together, but mostly to honor her. A few times, we met in Idaho, other times in California.

Grandchildren were more often likely to be present when they were still young, before they had jobs and families of their own. Before failing health slowed her down, Mother also came to California once or twice to visit my sister Chris, who had moved from Idaho after high school to attend college, and me. She also traveled abroad with church groups after my youngest sister grew up. Eventually she developed chronic obstructive pulmonary disease (COPD), and passed away from heart failure, very peacefully, still in her own home in Kellogg, on June 14, 1999.

Crawford Clan

* * * * *

The twenty-five years Leon and I spent on Edgeview Drive were filled with the usual amalgam of family events: Larry and Mary's graduation from high school and enrollment in college, each of the children's marriages, the birth of grandchildren, Leon's heart attack, recovery and therapy, and his knee replacement surgery. And, as is inevitable with age, we began to slow down.

Once we were both retired, Leon grew restless. With the exception of his stint in the army and his college years, he had lived in Pasadena all of his life. We were now empty-nesters with no grandchildren living nearby, and had no real reason to stay in Pasadena.

Pauline Crawford Crabb

Over the years, every place we traveled with the band, Leon would consider as a potential new home for us. Outside of Tucson, adjoining the Saguaro National Park in southern Arizona, we found a very inviting small house with a creek bed in the back yard. I inquired of someone in the area, "What do you do in the summer when it's so hot?" "Oh, we move away for three months," they replied. As well as being too far away from the children and grandchildren, Leon would not have been able to keep playing in the band. So that plan went awry. But he kept on looking.

We were already part-time residents of San Clemente. In 1990, we had bought a one-third interest in a small two-bedroom condo on Avenida Lobeiro, a narrow one-way street with direct access to the beach below. From our patio we could see the whitewater waves, and hear them breaking on the shore. Every third Friday, from noon to noon the next Friday, the condo was ours. Our partners in the condo were Nancy and Jack Clemens, and Kate and John Harris, long-time friends of ours. (Remember those names? We traveled with the Harris's to Europe in '74.)

When Leon's itch to move became ever stronger, we considered moving north to Eureka, where our son Larry lived. However, the rainy climate and frequent overcast days of the area dampened our enthusiasm for that location. Because we were spoiled by the location of our current condo, any place we bought, we decided, would have to have the ocean in sight. We looked around San Clemente, hoping to buy a place of our own. Most of the real estate we looked at was either beyond our price range, or in the category of a fixer-upper, which definitely did not appeal to us. The one condo we really liked, and which we thought we could afford, one situated above the municipal golf course with a view of the ocean on the horizon, was sold by the time we drove back to our condo to call the realtor. (We didn't own a cell phone in 1990.) Part-time status at the beach seemed to be our fate.

In June of 1999, when my mother passed away, I went to Kellogg for her funeral. After the services, my brother and I accompanied her body to Halfway, Oregon, where she was buried in the little cemetery next to her mother and grandmother. While I was gone, Leon attended the high school graduation of our granddaughter, Lindsay. With her mom and brother, Lindsay lived in Ramona, a town close to San Diego, just off of US Highway 15, about a two hour drive south of Pasadena.

On his way home from Ramona the next day after the graduation celebration, driving north on US 15, Leon was intrigued with the geology of the terrain, which looks like some Goliath with a gigantic shovel has thrown, helter-skelter, huge ochre-colored rocks into tall piles along the side of the road. The landscape gradually changes as you pass the small town of Temecula, but the atmosphere remains dry, almost desert-like. The smaller towns of Lake Elsinore and Murrieta, just north of Temecula, where a number of new housing developments were being built, also looked interesting and he made a short side trip to look at one of these tracts, just to check it out. He liked what he saw, but didn't describe any of it to me when I got back to Pasadena, because, he told me later, he was sure I wouldn't be interested in moving out to "the sticks."

Later that summer, the Golden Eagle Jazz Band was invited to play a gig at Solano Beach, a town almost due west from the Temecula area. I went along and we spent the night at a motel not far from where the band had played. The next morning after breakfast, Leon suggested we drive home inland by way of Interstate 15. He also suggested Murrieta looked like an interesting place to live. The prices were right, he informed me, compared to property values in Pasadena.

As we passed Temecula going north we kept an eye out for Open House signs and new tracts of homes. We saw not one real estate sign on the freeway until we came to Lake Elsinore. There, just beyond Railroad Canyon Road, our imagination was captured by an invitation to live in Tuscany Hills. A bit of Italy, right here in southern California. Tuscany Hills. It sounded so romantic.

We drove up Summerhill Road, and wended our way along several side streets at the top of the hill. We parked the car and went through one or two open houses. Most of the styles were really not to our liking, either too formal or too glitzy. I couldn't see our furniture in any of those rooms.

At the Bel Fiore Realty office we looked at a few scale models on tables around the small room, but none of these struck our fancy either.

"What I really want," I told the saleswoman, "is a view of the ocean."

"Well, we don't have an ocean, but I think we have just the view you would love," she said. "Come with me."

We got into her car, and she drove us a few blocks to a less than half-finished house. She opened the front door, and led us straight out into a small, totally unfinished, black rock-strewn backyard. From our vantage point, we looked down upon the red tiled roofs of the houses below. With a little imagination one might picture the hills of Tuscany. Beyond three or four terraces of houses lay Canyon Lake, a small man-made lake surrounded by new homes. It wasn't the ocean, but it was a view of peaceful blue water. In the distance we could see, what we later came to call, "our far mountains." You could see for miles and miles. You could almost see into tomorrow.

Back inside the shell of the house, the realtor described the plan of the developers, but she also informed us we could choose the flooring, the carpets, the window treatments, the kitchen appliances, even the bathroom fixtures, if we wanted something different from the original materials stipulated in the plan. She was offering us the choice of Ghirardelli or See's chocolates if we didn't like plain Hershey bars. It was very tempting.

"What do you think?" Leon asked me. I could see how much he wanted to make an offer right then and there. On our way back to the real estate office, the saleswoman described the advantages of living in a setting with a homeowners' association and all the amenities it offered: a pool, a club house, gardening and landscaping maintenance. We drove back to Pasadena with papers to sign, put our house up for sale within a few days, sold it quickly, and within sixty days moved from Pasadena, the city that had been our home for forty-three years, and Leon Dee's home for sixty-five years.

We moved to Lake Elsinore, a small town in the middle of nowhere.

Chapter 16 ...by Tuscany Hills

Between 1999 and 2005

Most people look to downsize after they retire. Less often means more. Less work—more time. Less house—more travel. Less yard—more playtime. Leon and I did just the opposite. From a one-story house we went to a two-story house. From three bedrooms we went to the equivalent of five bedrooms. To fill these rooms we had to buy more furniture. With the clarity of hindsight, it seems somewhat ludicrous to have taken this path, but at the time we weren't looking into the future, we were thoroughly engrossed in the present.

From our perspective, the move to Lake Elsinore was the culmination of our lives together. We started our married life at Idaho State College in a no-bedroom rental unit, facetiously called 'the rabbit hutches,' as I mentioned in an earlier chapter. As a reminder: It consisted of a kitchen with a coal-fed stove and an ice box which required a block of ice every three or four days. If we wanted a hot shower on a hot summer's day (or any day for that matter) we had to fuel the kitchen stove which, in turn, heated the water for the shower.

For forty-six years we had worked hard, studied hard, and raised our family in the best way we knew how. Our house in Tuscany Hills was the fulfillment of the American dream. Our dream. Even the name of the subdivision of the Tuscany Hills development, Bel Fiore, and the name of our street, Del Torino, gave us pleasure. For a relatively short time, we reveled in the benefits of our years of hard work.

I realize I'm not writing this chapter for anyone other than myself, so please bear with me while I return in my mind's eye to that little piece of Italy on a hill in southern California. I'm still emotionally tied to that house. It gives me such pleasure to remember the warmth and happiness in the home Leon and I shared there for three short years.

The design of the house was such that from your first step into the living area you could see past the family room to sliding glass doors which opened to the blue sky beyond our small yard. A kitchen window over the sink also overlooked the yard. As well as the living and dining areas on the first floor there was also a guest bedroom, a full bath and a wonderful laundry room that led to the garage. In our Pasadena house the washer and dryer sat out in the garage, so we didn't take this feature for granted.

A large master bedroom was on the second floor. A sliding glass door led to a small balcony which, like the family room and kitchen on the first floor, overlooked Canyon Lake and the mountains beyond. Because of its location, there was no need for window coverings, and our large mirrored dresser sat on an east-facing wall, catching the first rays of sunrise. We tended to wake with the dawn.

Also upstairs was a 16' x 20' unfinished loft where Leon installed a 4' x 8' piece of plywood on a couple of saw horses to hold his model electric train. The remainder of the space served as our art studio. Another room we called the library. It served as a second TV viewing area and could also sleep guests when needed. An office with *his* and *hers* desks sat across the hall, and, finally, there was a music room with all of Leon's stereo and recording components, as well as a treadmill. The house was beyond anything we had ever envisioned.

We took pleasure in selecting every detail that went into finishing the interior of the house: the tile, the carpets, the paint colors, the window treatments. With nothing more than sheer good luck on our part, from the yellow pages of the local telephone book, we called, interviewed and hired a semi-retired landscape architect to design the small backyard, which was nothing more than black rock when we moved in. Robert Weaver, as we came to learn, had designed a number of impressive corporate projects in southern California. He drew up plans for our very small area which made the most of its limited space. By creating a "sitting wall," using the same brick as we had installed in the family room hearth and fireplace, we could comfortably entertain a fairly large crowd. A lighted BBQ area was piped for a natural gas line. Weaver included a raised bed for herbs and vegetables, as well as an alcove for a terra cotta statue of St. Francis which we had picked up at a garden store in Temecula.

We did not want a lawn to mow, so Mr. Weaver had the patio floor laid with cement which was scored on the diagonal, mirroring the same pattern as the large tile in our informal dining area, creating a natural visual flow from inside to outside. On summer evenings, we sat outside, watching the shapes of the mountains recede in the distance, and the lights of the homes below us twinkle ever more brightly as dusk became night.

Because the entire development was relatively new, and several houses on our street were still under construction, many of the neighbors were also new to one another. Only a few days after we had moved in, we were coming out of the house one evening when we met two couples strolling down the sidewalk on our side of the street.

"Hello, and welcome," called out a tall, nice-looking, middle-aged man. "I'm Harold and this is Ginny, my wife," he said. "These are the Bells, Dr. Barkley and his wife, Vivian. We've just come from Alice's where we have a Bible study. Maybe you'd like to join us." We shook hands all around, expressing our 'nice-to-meet-yous' and thanked them for the invitation.

We decided, almost on the spot, this would be a wonderful way for us to get acquainted on our new street. Since I'd retired, I had been attending a Bible study at our parish church in Pasadena, enjoying it very much. Although he hadn't gone with me, Leon had watched some of the videos we'd viewed, and he and I had started reading the Bible after breakfast on those mornings we were at home. We thought it would be great if we could study the scriptures together. The next week we joined the group.

How we came to learn about watercolor classes offered in Fallbrook, I don't recall, but soon we were driving down to Fallbrook once a week to paint under the tutelage of Mary Thomaskevitch, whose work we came to admire. Our circle of friends widened.

Fortune smiled on us in another aspect. In the small adjacent community of Wildomar, we found a highly recommended physician, Dr. Purnima Patel, who became our family doctor. She had a reputation of being the physician to whom other physicians sent their families.

We had absolute confidence her ability to look out for our physical wellbeing.

As well as the spiritual nourishment we received in our Bible study, we became members of the St. Francis of Rome Catholic Church community. We liked the small church atmosphere and Father Robert Guerrero, the pastor, was very personable. Shortly after we got settled, he came and blessed our new home. I later facilitated a Bible study in the parish.

Our move from Pasadena didn't mean Leon had to give up playing the New Orleans jazz he loved so much. Lake Elsinore was less than an hour's drive from Steamers, a small café in Fullerton where the Golden Eagle Jazz Band was now playing their gig almost every other Sunday afternoon. And, it wasn't long before he had joined another group, the Second Street Jazz Band, which played on a regular basis in Escondido.

Jazz was still a major factor in our lives in the year 2000. We must have put hundreds, if not thousands of miles of jazz-related travel on our calendar. Most of the jazz festivals to which the band was invited to play were in the our own country, but in July, 2000, after a quick trip to Hailey, Idaho to celebrate my 50th high school reunion, we spent the rest of the month in Italy, much of that time traveling with the Ken and Flossie Smith, prior to a Golden Eagle gig in Varese, a small town, a forty-five minute train ride northwest from Milan.

One evening at the Hotel Albergo, high up on a mountain above the small town of Tremezzo where we were staying before going on to Varese, Leon and I sat together on the small balcony of our room, overlooking the placid, deep blue water of Lake Como. The village lights of Bellagio twinkled in the distance. One of us asked the other, "Did you ever think, when we were going to ISC and living in Pocatello, we'd ever be doing *this*?" It was just the little girl from Idaho talking to the little boy from Kansas, sharing a magical moment. We were incredulous, and never really took our good fortune for granted.

* * * * *

It's hard to say just when Leon's health problems seriously began to limit our comings and goings. He had been under a cardiologist's care ever since his first heart attack in 1982, but with rehab he seemed to have recovered, although he had also been diagnosed with diabetes. In December, 1998, he had knee replacement surgery, and that slowed him down somewhat. I don't recall our first year on Del Torino being marked by bouts of illness, although he was seeing Dr. Patel on a regular basis for his diabetes.

In 2001 we sailed on a Renaissance cruise that took us to Tahiti, Indonesia, Bali, Java, Lombok and Komodo. As beautiful as Tahiti and Bali were, I thought to myself, *We should have been here ten years ago. Then we would have reveled in the romance of the islands.* We enjoyed ourselves, but Leon missed a side trip to Borobudur, an ancient Buddhist temple in central Java, as he wasn't feeling well enough that day to join our excursion.

My weekly calendars for 2001 and 2002 are missing from my collection, but I recall more and more frequent appointments with Dr. Patel.

The last photo I have of the whole family gathered together was taken on Christmas Day, 2001. We are standing in the front yard of our house. Leon and I are wearing sweatshirts that Tracy had given us years before when the grandkids were little. Across the front of each sweatshirt are palm prints. Our granddaughter Lindsay's are on mine, and grandson Jeffrey's decorate Leon's. In our picture, Jeffrey is already taller than his dad and has very short hair. Ryan, standing with his arms around his sister, Hannah, was a college student at Harvey Mudd at the time. He's sporting blue hair. Both of our sons and our son-in-law are sporting moustaches. Mary's two children, Vikki and Steven, the youngest grandchildren, are still in grade school. It was a happy day. We announced at the dinner table we would take the whole family to Hawaii on our 50th wedding anniversary, in the summer of 2003. It was probably more my idea than my husband's, but that was the plan.

I don't remember the month or the day in 2002 when Leon said to me, "I just can't play in the band anymore. I can't keep up." His energy was flagging. Making the decision to leave the band was probably one of the hardest things he ever had to do.

Even harder, and more devastating, was the day Leon had to give up driving. Because of his health condition, he needed a doctor's signature to renew his driver's license before his birthday in November. None of his physicians would agree to give permission. We traded in the Lincoln Continental he really loved driving, but which had become more and more difficult for him to get in and out of, and bought a six-passenger 2001 Toyota Sienna with 17,500 miles on it, hoping perhaps we could take it on a trip. (We loved our road trips almost as much as those to more distant destinations.) We planned to lower the back seats to make a bed for him to lie down on when he got tired. He never once drove the Sienna. And we never took that road trip.

In October, 2002, Leon said to me, as we were lying in bed one night, "I want to become a full Catholic." I am sure it was then he knew he was not going to regain his health. From the time the children were little, he had always gone to church with me, and I had never pressured him to convert to my religion. On the contrary, after we had moved to Lake Elsinore, and I had recognized his health was failing, I had asked him if he would like to go to another of the Protestant churches in the area. He said he liked our little church. When he made his desire of wanting to become a Catholic known to me, I tried to tell him it wasn't necessary. I wanted him to feel, when it was time for him to go home to God, he would be embraced, no matter what religious denomination he professed. But he persisted, and within a few days I called Father Guerrero, explained Leon's wishes, and asked him if he could come over to our house. Father was ready to anoint Leon that day, but Leon insisted he didn't 'know enough,' and wanted more time to prepare. For a short while, a friend from our church came to the house, brought reading materials and explained more of the background of the Catholic faith. Some days Leon really didn't feel up to having company. She would then give me the material she'd brought, and I would go over the topic with him. We really didn't ever have any long conversations about his dying, but some evenings, in bed, Leon would say to me, "Pray with me, and bless me."

Toward the end of 2002, the guest room on the first floor became our bedroom as Leon was having trouble going up the stairs each night. (*It's so hard to write about this period. I want to skip it altogether, but feel compelled to continue.*) As Leon grew weaker I did whatever was necessary to make our lives as normal as possible. When you have loved someone for so many years it is, as Scripture says, "the two shall be as one," and you do what you can to help the other in whatever way possible.

New Year's Day, 2003. My calendar reads: *Leon to hospital.* It was a short stay as I recall, but I note more and more frequent entries with the same message. When he became too weak to get to Dr. Patel's office, she suggested the time had come for us to contact a nearby

Hospice group who would provide us with all the medical care we needed to keep Leon comfortable. Although it went unsaid, we knew what this meant.

Hospice provided a home health worker, a physical therapist, and a registered nurse who not only saw to Leon's needs but encouraged me as well. One afternoon, as I was walking with her to her car at the end of her shift, the nurse said to me, "You've been given the wonderful privilege of walking Leon home to God." She recognized the signs his time with us would not be long. She also told me if our son, who lived in northern California, wanted to have a good conversation with his dad he should come soon. As soon as she left, I went back into the house and called Larry who flew down from Arcata two days later.

On February fourth, Father Guerrero came to the house to anoint Leon, and receive him into the Catholic Church. Jean Powell, our neighbor, who shared our faith, and whom we loved, had agreed to be Leon's sponsor. As I led Father into our bedroom, he asked Jean and me to leave for a while so he and Leon could have some privacy. Within a short while, Father called us back in, and, following the rites of the Catholic Church, anointed Leon with the chrism oil used for Confirmation, welcoming him into the church. Next, Father anointed him a second time, reciting the prayers dedicated to strengthen him through his time of suffering. Leon then received the Eucharist for the first time, and he seemed to be very much at peace.

That night, in bed, just before we went to sleep, Leon said to me, "I know I'm going to a better place." Then, he continued, "and you'll do your thing." Whatever he meant by that comment I don't know. He didn't go into it any further. I didn't ask. I've always hoped it meant he had confidence I would be okay.

Leon was spending most of his days in bed now, and the only window in our guest room looked out onto our neighbor's barren sidewall. The room darkened by early afternoon. Because we had such a beautiful view of Canyon Lake and the blue skies from our family room, we had a hospital bed brought in, and moved Leon into the brighter, airier setting.

Together we could watch our favorite TV shows, and he could see me in the kitchen as I fixed our meals or puttered around. In the evenings he could enjoy the fire in the fireplace. I slept on the sofa across from his bed, so I would be able to hear him if he wakened in the night. Each day either a nurse from Hospice or a volunteer would come to help with his caregiving. Whenever I needed to go to the store or pick up a prescription, someone was always at the house to watch over my husband.

Over the next week and weekend all the children and grandchildren who lived in southern California came to visit. Ken and Flossie Smith drove down, and, just like old times, Ken and Leon joked about something. Kate and John Harris also stopped by. Even one of the Golden Eagle jazz fans asked to come over. Larry would often play the small spinet piano we had bought when we first moved here, and Leon enjoyed listening to familiar tunes.

Although it was midweek, on Wednesday, February twelfth, two days before Valentine's Day, our son Leon drove up from his home in San Diego, and Mary drove down from Glendora to see their dad and visit with Larry.

The kids and I barbecued steaks. As we sat at the little round table in the dining area, across from Leon's bed, we ate and talked and played Golden Eagle tapes. We all could see Leon's right hand, ever so slightly, strumming to the beat of his own banjo. As I recall, it

211

was a happy evening, recounting stories and memories, each talking a little about his or her work. A few glasses of wine helped lighten the mood around the table.

In the middle of the night, Leon became very restless. I got up and gave him a tiny dose of the medication he took to keep him comfortable. The restlessness continued, and I couldn't get back to sleep. At six-thirty, as the first rays of the sun streamed through the window, I got up and called the Hospice number. I identified myself and told the voice at the other end of the line how restless Leon seemed to be. She said it would be okay to give him a little more of the medication, which I did. It seemed to help calm his fretfulness.

Around eight o'clock that morning, the phone rang. The Hospice volunteer for the day called to tell me she was having car trouble, and wouldn't be able to come to the house until she got her car situation under control. After I hung up the phone, I walked back to Leon's bed. He was lying ever so peacefully. No pain showed in his face. No anxiety. I knew at once he had gone home to God. Whether it was then or later, I don't recall, but at some point, I could see, in my mind's eye, my husband being carried in the arms of Jesus. On my daily calendar, in slanting penmanship across the space for Thursday, February 13, I have written in blue ink: *Leon went home to God! We loved you so much!*

I have always been so grateful there were no strangers in our home that morning. I've also thought perhaps it wasn't just mere coincidence that the volunteer couldn't keep her date with us. Who knows? But, it was so good for me to have that last time alone with my husband.

* * * * *

As I write of this last day with my husband, my heart tells me to include a little poem I've cherished for so many years, one I found in the small grey-covered book of poetry I bought as a teenager. It describes how I felt about Leon Dee Crabb, and it belongs to my story.

"*Love*" by Roy Croft

I love you,
Not only for what you are,
But for what I am
When I am with you.

I love you,
Not only for what
You have made of yourself,
But for what
You are making of me.

I love you
For the part of me
That you bring out;
I love you
For putting your hand
Into my heaped-up heart
And passing over
All the foolish, weak things
That you can't help
Dimly seeing there,
And for drawing out
Into the light
All the beautiful belongings
That no one else had looked
Quite far enough to find.

I love you because you
Are helping me to make
Of the lumber of my life
Not a tavern
But a temple;

Pauline Crawford Crabb
Out of the works
Of my every day
Not a reproach
But a song.

I love you
Because you have done
More than any creed
Could have done
To make me good,
And more than any fate
Could have done
To make me happy.

You have done it
Without a touch,
Without a word,
Without a sign.
You have done it
By being yourself,
Perhaps that is what
Being a friend means,
After all.

A friend, a husband, a lover. Unlike the final stanza of this poem, there was a touch; there were many words; there were many signs. Each helped me grow into the person I have become. I was blessed to be able to share my life with this man.

Although more than ten years have passed, many of the details of the next few weeks, and the next few months are still keenly etched in my memory. But there are no 'what-ifs' or 'if onlys' I rue. No regrets—other than wishing we'd had more time together.

* * * * *

214

The usual formalities that accompany a death in the family were addressed. Within the week, my sister, Sharon, and her son, Tim, and daughter-in-law, Cindy, arrived, as did the rest of Larry's family. The evening before the funeral Mass at St. Francis of Rome, a rosary for Leon was said in the mortuary chapel.

I had asked our sons and son-in-law, as well as the three grandsons, to be pallbearers at the funeral. When we all arrived at the church, Larry's daughter, Hannah, asked why none of the girls were pallbearers. She wanted to be a part of the procession and walk with the others, guiding her grandfather's casket down the center aisle. I saw no reason why she shouldn't. And so she did, walking between the men and boys at the end of the casket as it was brought to the front of the church. I was proud of her.

Later that afternoon, the family and a few close friends met at the Mountain View Cemetery in Altadena where Leon was laid to rest, not six feet distant from the grave of his father, Leon Ezra Crabb, who had died in 1943. An honor guard carried the casket to the burial site, and he was lowered into the ground while his long-time friend, Ken Smith, blew taps on his cornet. Father Walter, a priest from our former parish church in Pasadena, led us in prayer and blessed the grave. Afterwards, the family and friends drove out to Glendora to have dinner at Mary and Dan's house.

* * * * *

Lake Elsinore was too far for many of Leon's school and work associates to come for a funeral service, and we wanted the burial to be just for the family and very few close friends. So on the last Saturday of March we held a Celebration of Life service at the Sierra Madre Community Center, only a few miles from where Leon had worked for over thirty years. Because New Orleans music was so much a part of Leon's life, this setting and service lent itself to the happy memories of the years he spent working in the San Gabriel School District and playing jazz with a number of music groups, most especially the Golden Eagle Jazz Band.

Two Kiwanis pastor-friends of Leon's began and ended the service with their prayers. Mary and I worked with Ken Smith to coordinate the music we wanted, and Ken called upon a number of musicians, who played several sets. Superintendent Gary Goodson, from the school district, and several family members and friends paid tribute to Leon as a father, grandfather, co-worker and musician. The ambience was joyful. I loved hearing the stories told and the familiar chords of the tunes that Leon had played so many times. Some of my colleagues from Pasadena City College as well as Leon's cohorts from San Gabriel attended. Both my younger sisters, Chris and Terry, were there as well. It couldn't have been a better afternoon.

After the last guest had departed, our son, Leon, drove me from Sierra Madre back to our house at Lake Elsinore. It had been a long day, standing in new shoes, greeting and chatting with family and friends. I went upstairs to bed, absolutely exhausted. In the middle of the night my right leg began to cramp with a terrible Charlie horse. I got up and tried to walk to the bathroom. Then my other leg cramped as well. I was in excruciating pain, and writhed on the floor for a long time. I was afraid to cry out or complain. The scenario that took place in my head was one in which my family decided, because I had this debilitating condition, they really couldn't let me live alone. It sounds ridiculous now, but as a new widow I was infantile in my thinking. I prayed and prayed, hard and long. Gradually the cramps subsided and I was able to get back to sleep. I woke the next morning totally exhausted.

Nothing really ever gets 'back to normal' when adversity strikes, whether it be death, separation, or a debilitating illness. Life will never be the same as it was before. But somehow we learn to adjust, or rather *I* learned to adjust. Of course there were tears. And more tears. A biblical phrase speaking of "the orphans and the widows" kept coming up in my mind. Now I was one of those widows.

But, as one of my art friends said to me, during the first year after Leon was gone, "Eventually, the sharp corners round off." And my daughter's reminder, as I was probably feeling sorry for myself one day, "Mother, you know you aren't the only widow in the world," also helped. Rather than be resentful, that advice helped me put things in perspective.

However, about three months into my new widowhood I was feeling very depressed, and decided I should take advantage of a grief group that was offered by the same Hospice organization which had helped me in Leon's last illness. I called to see when the meetings were scheduled, took courage, and drove myself over to Menifee, a town just a few minutes from our house. I don't remember the details of the first meeting, but do know I found it helpful, and the next week I returned. This time, as we were getting ready to begin a session, a younger woman walked in with an older man.

"Is there anyone here who might be able to take my father home today?" she asked. "He doesn't live very far from here," she continued. "I have a doctor's appointment and I'm not sure just when I'll be out of there."

I thought to myself, "No one's home waiting for me," so I raised my hand and offered, "I can do it."

Pauline Crawford Crabb

At the end of the session Jim, or whatever his name was (I don't remember), got into my Sienna, and gave me directions to his house. During the short drive, I learned a lot about him. He was a Catholic (and so was I). He loved Dixieland music (and so did I). He loved to dance (and so did I). By the time I dropped him off at his house, and learned we had so many things in common, I was afraid he might ask me to go out with him. It was probably the last thing from his mind, but, as a consequence, I never went back to the grief group again. Somehow my depression dissipated with time, and I've laughed about that incident many times in the years since.

Without the grief group, I found one way to assuage my melancholy was through writing. I didn't write every day, but, when I was stressed, I found the very physical act of typing on the keyboard, and re-reading my thoughts and feelings put into printed words, was very helpful. Not long ago I came across a poem I wrote in the spring of 2004. It has no title.

It's hard to go from a 'we' to a 'me,'
When for so long I thought less of me
And more of thee.
It's hard to think of 'my' and 'mine,'
When for so long I thought of 'our' and 'thine.'
I am,
You were,
I'm here,
You're there.
Does love compact from two to one?
What is left when day is done?
It's easy to say, but harder to know,
My love of the Lord must ever grow,
Until one day I'll no longer be me,
But once again united with thee.

Perhaps not great poetry, yet these words illustrate the difficulty I was having with expressing *mine* instead of *ours.* Almost fifty years of being *us,* made it a challenge just to think of *me.* Overall, though, I think I was doing a pretty good job of making the necessary adjustments to a single life, to widowhood. Our friends on Del Torino, friends from St. Frances of Rome, friends from the music circle, friends from my book club, and friends from our art associations all helped me make that transition.

* * * * *

In the fall of 2003, I went on a pilgrimage with my church to Portugal and France, where we visited the shrines of Our Lady of Fatima and Our Lady of Lourdes. This was a disappointing trip for me. Unfortunately, being a neophyte in my new single life, I had agreed to be a roommate with an older woman, who often was not able to keep up with the group. The tour leader, more or less, assigned me the role of *ad hoc* caretaker, which I resented immensely. I thought to myself, *Here I am on a Christian pilgrimage and I don't feel very Christian at all.*

The following year I took a river cruise from Moscow to St. Petersburg. A former Parent Ed teacher/friend had agreed to be my roommate on this cruise, but, at the last minute, had to cancel for health reasons. Additionally, a friend from the Temecula book club, the woman who had persuaded me to go on this trip in the first place, also cancelled. Her reason? A fear of being mugged in a Russian subway. I thought about backing out as well, but decided against it. (As I wrote earlier, my father had worked in Russia before he was married, and I had always wanted to go there.)

The Russian adventure was the first trip I took on my own, and I got along very well. There were several other single women on the tour with whom I made friends. This included one with whom I later shared an apartment in

Florence, Italy, in 2010, while we both took classes in Renaissance art classes offered through a local California community college.

* * * * *

I was building my life anew, and would have been content to live in my beautiful dream home at 16 Del Torino, had it not been for a fateful phone call I got one afternoon in the spring of 2005, from our good friend, John Harris. He and Kate, Leon's former secretary at Washington School, had been the couple who invited Leon and me to become partners in the condo in San Clemente in 1990.

John was not only our friend; he was also a real estate agent. He called to tell me Jack and Nancy Clemens wanted to sell their share of condo we owned together. John said he and Kate also wanted to sell. I was overwhelmed. John went on to tell me to think about the situation for a few days, and then get back to him.

The short version of the story is that I made up my mind I did not want to sell my share of the condo. I felt there might never be another chance to live so close to the beach. Even more than my husband, I feel a kinship with that huge body of water, the Pacific Ocean. After talking it over with my children, I decided to put 16 Del Torino on the market, and buy the remaining two-thirds shares of the condo from my partners.

I would make San Clemente my new hometown.

Christmas 2001 – Our last family photo

Chapter 17 ...by the Spanish Village by the Sea

It seems a little ironic that more than seventy-five years after my mother wrote of a little town she passed through on a bus from Kellogg, Idaho to attend college in San Diego, California, I should be living *"in San Clemente* [where, as she wrote to her mother] *all the houses are white stucco houses with red tile roofs. It is more like a resort right on the beach or near there..."*

Of course, times have changed, but the vision of Ole Hansen, founder of the city of San Clemente, being a little Spanish village by the sea still holds true with many of the city's inhabitants. Only a short segment of the roadway my mother traveled on, the road that ran close to the beach, remains today. It has been mainly replaced by US Interstate 5, which runs north and south, splaying the town from top to bottom like a broken zipper. Newer developments now extended east into the canyons.

Making the transition from our beautiful new home in the Tuscany Hills of Lake Elsinore to living full-time in my small two-bedroom condo, built in 1976, with all the attending ailments of its age, was far more traumatic than I could ever have imagined.

In the first place, other than the 'rabbit hutches' Dee and I first inhabited as newlyweds at Idaho State College in Pocatello, I had never lived in an apartment. Other than the shanty in Santo Tomas during WWII, my family and I had always lived in a house, small though it might have been, but separate from our neighbors, with a yard of our own. While raising our family, each of our homes had been a little larger than the one we left. To move from a five-bedroom, two-story house overlooking a lake and the far mountains into a small two-bedroom condo, with neighbors on either side and on top of me, was, I thought, for the first six to eight months in San Clemente, a terrible mistake. A mistake I couldn't correct because my beautiful home in Lake Elsinore had been sold.

One of the comments I resented most, when spoken by a family member, friend or even a casual acquaintance, was, "With just one person, you don't need such a big house anymore." I thought to myself, *Who are you to tell me what I need? You don't live in this tiny, cluttered* (even with an additional storage unit to hold the overflow) *condo. Don't tell me what I need.* Occasionally, I spoke my mind aloud. I missed my big house terribly. The first summer was exceptionally painful because the unit above me was rented by a single mom with two teenage daughters who played their music so loudly the ceiling in my office/art room shuddered.

In 2006, as a new resident of San Clemente, I knew only one person: Anne Johnson. She had, as I wrote earlier, been a friend of my husband and matron of honor at our wedding. Now a widow, Anne and I resumed our friendship and she helped me put me in touch with the few medical professionals which everyone at our age needs to be acquainted with. Anne doesn't drive at night, and doesn't like to drive at all, so I'm the designated driver when we go out. It is comforting to still be in touch with someone who was a friend of Dee.

Also comforting, and helping me make the adjustment to San Clemente, was a group of people from my church, Our Lady of Fatima Catholic Church, which sits upon a low hill overlooking the ocean. Although Leon and I had been going to Mass at Our Lady of Fatima (OLF) during the weekends we spent in San Clemente, we had not established any friendships or real connection with the parishioners. After I moved, I made a conscious decision to become involved with the parish in some way, thereby giving me an attachment both to the church and to the town. I volunteered to be on the Hospitality Committee which serves coffee and donuts after the Masses each Sunday. That same spring I took a course on the history of the Church held at OLF taught by a woman named Kathy Schinhofen. I admired her broad scope of knowledge and the depth of her faith. I hoped to be able to get to know her better.

One morning after class, I approached Kathy. "I was involved in my churches in Pasadena and Lake Elsinore," I said. "Is there any way I could be of help here?" She suggested I become a part of the RCIA (Rite of Christian Initiation of Adults) team. I started attending their meetings every Tuesday evening, and helped Kathy prepare those adults who had yet to receive the sacrament of Confirmation. When she left OLF to take another position, I took on that ministry.

Thus began a closer relationship not only with my church, but I also began to develop a sense of belonging to the community of San Clemente as a whole. During my second year here I joined the San Clemente Art Association, which gave me another avenue to meet people and become involved. Before long I had a position on their Board. It gave me a purpose and sense of being cared about.

Oscar Wilde wrote, "The consciousness of loving and being loved brings a warmth and richness to life that nothing else can bring." Until I became a widow, I think I may have taken 'being loved' for granted. After February 13, 2003, when the love of my life left me, everything changed.

Actually, if we think much about it, life is nothing but a series of changes. Now, at eighty, these changes seem to come about fast and furiously. Perhaps it is because our son Leon, only fifty-eight years old, died in June of this year after only five days in a hospital, I am more aware of the tenuousness of life. There are no free passes, no 'Get out of jail' tickets, no guarantees for a set number of days or years. What is guaranteed is that I can choose to appreciate my life in this little town of San Clemente and to be a part of the community, which will bring, as Oscar Wilde said, "a warmth and richness" to my life.

I have just finished reading the story of Helen Keller, a truly admirable human being. Although she was blind, deaf and mute, with assistance, primarily that of Anne Sullivan, her teacher, she rose above her disabilities, became well educated, and worked tirelessly on behalf of the blind. One of her quotations struck a chord with me. She said, "Security is mostly a superstition. It does not exist in nature, nor do the children of men as a whole experience it. Avoiding danger is no safer in the long run than outright exposure. Life is either a daring adventure, or nothing."

My son, Larry, sent me a birthday card a few years ago with a shortened version of the same quote on the cover: *Life is either a daring adventure, or nothing.* Moving to San Clemente did not seem like a daring adventure, but perhaps the adventure comes with how I spend my coming days, weeks, months, and perhaps even years.

When I was in high school I had a crush on a very popular, very handsome boy in my class. He loved poetry, and among his favorites was *Thanatopsis* by William Cullen Bryant. It seems sort of ridiculous in retrospect, but I memorized the entire poem just to impress him. Oh, what we do in the name of puppy love.

Most of the lines have faded from memory, but as I write this chapter of *My Life Defined* I think of Bryant's advice as he wrote in the last stanza of "*Thanatopsis*":

> *So live, that when thy summons comes to join*
> *The innumerable caravan which moves*
> *To that mysterious realm, where each shall take*
> *His chamber in the silent halls of death,*
> *Thou go not, like the quarry-slave at night,*
> *Scourged to his dungeon, but sustained and soothed*
> *By an unfaltering trust, approach thy grave*
> *Like one who wraps the drapery of his couch*
> *About him, and lies down to pleasant dreams.*

My faith tells me that Bryant's description of the "*chamber in the silent halls of death*" may not be exactly what I hope to experience, but I do want to go, wherever the path leads, "*sustained and soothed by an unfaltering trust, like one who wraps the drapery of his couch about him, and lies down to pleasant dreams.*"

From the patio of my condo here in San Clemente, this little Spanish village by the sea, I can see the ocean's waves, sometimes softly, sometimes pounding, always with rhythmic regularity, wash upon the shore only to be drawn back into the broad expanse of water which reaches farther than my eye can see. As I walk down the short path to the little park adjacent to our building to see the glow of the sunsets, I believe I am right where I should be. Right where God intended me to be.

My Life Defined...

When I walk close to the shore, or across the sand, with the fresh, salty breeze filling my nostrils, I feel at one with God's creation. I am filled with a sense of peace.

Occasionally, I come face to face with a friend.

I am no longer a stranger in this place.

Chapter 18 ...by Friends

"Friendship"
Oh, the comfort—the inexpressible comfort of feeling
safe with a person
 Having neither to weigh thoughts,
 Nor measure words—but pouring them
 All right out—just as they are—
  Chaff and grain together—
 Certain that a faithful hand will
 Take and sift them—
 Keep what is worth keeping—
 And with the breath of kindness
 Blow the rest away.
Dinah Maria Mulock Craik

This poem also comes from *Best Loved Poems*, the cherished book I've had since I was fifteen years old in Kellogg, Idaho. These days I keep it wrapped in a plastic bag. Its spine has disintegrated and its yellowing pages are brittle and torn, but whenever I think of friends who have helped define my life, the words of this poem speak most often to my heart.

My Life Defined...

Unlike my children, who went all through their school years with some of the same friends, I do not have a link to many friends from my early years. My friend, Joan Helble, whom I have known since I was four years old, is my only link with the years I spent in the Philippines. While I did not see her for the next eleven years, we corresponded all during that time, with the exception of the war years. With Joan I feel a strong thread of friendship woven through the fabric of our lives. Whenever we meet, we can sit comfortably in our rocking chairs just quietly, serenely enjoying the present company.

Because our family lived only four years in Triumph, Idaho, while I was going to high school in Hailey, and because I lived twelve miles out of town, I always had to make special arrangements to get together with my high school friends. Somehow, my friendships during those years were casual, not the close bonds of children who had grown up together. Consequently, while I enjoy seeing my classmates at those times I return to the area, I don't have a potpourri of warm memories to share with them.

Following our college years, when Leon and I moved to Nevada, and later to California, we were busy raising a family, going to school, and focusing on careers. We kept up with a few of our college friends, but as the years ran on, even these friends became fewer and fewer as we gradually lost touch with most of them.

Throughout our years in Pasadena, we had several circles of friends, mainly people connected with Leon's work in San Gabriel, or with his music activities. He had a few friends from his early school days, but many of them had moved away. We made a few close friends with the parents of our children's friends in the neighborhood.

Pauline Crawford Crabb

We had good times with all of them, but, again, they were the icing on the cake,

Friends were icing on the cake, yes, but not the substance of the cake itself. Friends were a category of people who formed an outer circle of relationships, a cushion of camaraderie or comfort, you might say. We did not rely on them to sustain us. Although we enjoyed their company, had many good times together, they were acquaintances or companions in some casual way. Some were peers with whom I worked, who I might call 'weekday' friends.

We made new friends when we moved to Lake Elsinore. We joined a neighborhood Bible study, met people in our cul-de-sac, others through our church, and still others when Leon joined another musical group, the Second Street Band, with whom he played regularly until he became ill.

The role of friends, however, changed dramatically for me once I became a widow. Friends became my link to the world beyond my house in Lake Elsinore, and, later, beyond my condo in San Clemente.

Although I have a loving family, all of them lead lives of their own, just as Leon and I led lives of our own for many years. Family members always include me in their celebrations. They invite and welcome me into their homes. They love me and they show their love. But, ultimately, I must return to my condo by myself. This is when I am sustained and nourished by friends. In the eight years that I've lived here in San Clemente, I've made friends from my church and friends who are in the art association. There are also professional acquaintances around town who welcome me when we meet. Beyond San Clemente, I have artist friends, and friends with whom I travel. Though casual, I have made friends in my writers' group. Each person contributes to my sense of wellbeing. I feel blessed by their company.

Although there is danger in naming specific people, and committing a sin of omission by not naming others, I would be remiss should I neglect to mention a few special friends who have certainly, on an ongoing basis, enriched my life these past few years.

There is Anne, who was my only attendant at our wedding, sixty years ago. She is a link to my husband, and she was the only person I knew when I moved to San Clemente. Ken and Flossie of the Golden Eagle Jazz Band, and who were our traveling companions for many years, have been my connection with a past life in music circles that were so important at the time. I know I'm always welcome in their home, day or night. Jean Knoblauch is another friend connected to the music world I once knew.

And, there is also Pam, who graciously welcomed me, with an offer of wine and cheese, the first week I moved into the condo eight years ago, and who helped make me feel more at home in my new surroundings. We are not of the same generation, but somehow that doesn't seem to matter. There are members of my book club, too many to name (but they know who they are), who always welcome me with open arms and open hearts. Each of these friends, in his or her own way, helps me be glad that I now live in San Clemente, this 'Spanish village by the sea.' These are friends about whom the words of the poem, "Friendship," were spoken.

However, with friends as with the family, when get-togethers or trips near or far come to an end, there again arrives the time when I must return to my condo by myself. As I insert the key into the front door lock, open it, and step inside, I nearly always call out, "Hi, House, I'm home. Did you miss me?" The house (it may be a condo, but I think of it as a house, as my home) and I are good friends. It shelters me, gives me warmth and a place to lay my weary head at the end of a day. Within its walls are all the mementos I need to be reminded of love and friendship—that of family, and that of friends.

One last thing. I believe the spirit of God graces these rooms. I am never alone. My faith tells me that He is truly my best friend.

Chapter 19 ...by Faith

"Faith"

From afar I watched a kite soar high in the sky,
A simple flat plate with a streaming tail.
I understood it to be tethered to earth,
But no line could I see.
I questioned not its tether, and yet I wondered:
Why couldn't it have been secured from on high,
By an unseen line which might draw it closer to the
world
Which none on earth can see?

To define my life in terms of ancestry and history is one thing; ancestry and history are created of fabric, comprised, more or less, of black and white facts, although I can't deny there are also shades of grey. Perhaps there are even holes and tears in the fabric of history, details best left to the imagination. For the most part, ancestry and history are the more concrete building blocks of a person's life.

However, to define my life by 'faith' is not only amorphous, it is an ever-changing, continually emerging facet of my being. In truth, now that I'm eighty (and it's been very hard for me to acknowledge that fact), I'm a little less ready to share this aspect of my life, and a little more reluctant to be called to task when beliefs and actions may not always seem congruent. But to disregard the spiritual aspect of its existence in my life story seems not only cowardly, it also denies what I believe is the core of my being.

I have been writing bits and pieces of this chapter, defining my life by faith, for many years, never bringing it to a conclusion that I might want to see in print for anyone—family, friend or stranger—to read. I'm not sure where to start. It isn't my purpose to write a thesis in defense of my faith, nor a discourse on my belief in Christianity. I'll leave that for others. Nor is it my purpose to find fault with others who do not share my beliefs. I only want to write about what I know, in my heart, is right for me.

In re-reading the material I wrote more than ten years ago, it is interesting for me to note that my earlier focus was on the institutionalized aspect of my religion, that of Roman Catholicism. I wrote about my mother assuring I was baptized and nurtured in her faith. I described the black and white photo of myself and my friend, Joan, which sits on my nightstand, each in her First Holy Communion dress. I recounted how I was adamant about being married in a Catholic church, and raising our children in the Church. I wrote of our daughter's miraculous (I believe) release by her kidnapper. I even talked about how my husband and I became ever more prayerful toward the ends of our lives.

What I did not always include in that writing were those times when I *felt* the presence of a loving God, a God whom I trust with my life, a personal God, an everyday God, and a God who sent his son, Jesus, to be my guide.

My Life Defined...

The everyday God I recognize and worship was shared by my husband very early in our marriage. I recall praying grace together as we sat down at the yellow chrome dinette table to eat our first dinner in our new apartment in Las Vegas, where Leon had taken his first teaching job. It felt just the right way for us to begin our new life in a new town. The strength we received through the sharing of prayers deepened our faith as we grew old together. For most of our later married lives we knelt at our bedside nightly before turning out the lights and calling it a day.

Many, many years ago, for Christmas in 1963, Leon gave me a copy of a small book entitled *The Practice of the Presence of God* by Brother Lawrence, a lay brother of the barefooted Carmelites in Paris in the mid-seventeenth century. It recounts how Brother Lawrence lived most simply, often among the pots and pans of a kitchen, where, in his words, *he might perform all his actions for the love of God.* My mother, who probably never heard of Brother Lawrence, also taught me a similar prayer, which she would say upon rising: *Everything I do today I do for the honor and glory of God.*

I do not recall being particularly aware of a personal relationship with God the Father, Jesus, or even the Holy Ghost, as we called the Holy Spirit, when I was growing up. My church attendance, while regular, was probably rather perfunctory. As St. Paul said to the Corinthians, "When I was a child, I spoke as a child, I understood as a child, I thought as a child. But, when I became a man, I put away the things of a child." Although, from another verse in the New Testament, Jesus says, "Let the children come to me, and do not prevent them; for the kingdom of heaven belongs to such as these." And so, with child-like faith I came to believe.

Pauline Crawford Crabb

In Pasadena, when we lived on South Grand Oaks Avenue, we belonged to St. Philip's Church on Hill Avenue. Our daughter was baptized there. That is where our boys went to primary school, and where we attended Mass on Sunday mornings. After the children were enrolled in school, my husband began accompanying us to church each week.

Whether it was on a Sunday morning with the whole family around me, or another time when I had been at Mass by myself, I had what I'll call a 'spiritual experience.' I described it, years later, in a journal I was keeping.

June 22, 2006 – Many, many years ago as I knelt in a pew at St. Philip's Church in Pasadena, I heard distinctly, as real as any voice has ever spoken to me, in a soft, yet firm voice, "Be kind and gentle and charitable, and all things will come to you." *There is no doubt in my mind that God was speaking just to me. I went home and wrote it on a slip of paper because I did not want to ever forget that promise.*

Just this past year I decided it was time to frame that little slip of paper with its fading blue ink, which is so apt to become lost or tossed if I don't protect it. *Kind—gentle—charitable—*isn't that what God is all about?

In the Catholic Church, we often speak of the 'Sacred Mysteries.' Although theologians have many answers, there are some questions for which there is no assurance other than that which unwavering faith provides. And sometimes our/my faith wavers. It must have been just such a time, March 23, 1986, when I wrote the following:

"How Can It Be?"

As I knelt in prayer
And gazed at the Host,
I asked myself, "How can it be?"
The glory of God, the fullness of Life,

My Life Defined...
In that one small host?

Then a vision of a sequestered Upper Room
Recalled the words of Jesus, as he held
Aloft a piece of bread, "This is my body."
And a low, but distinct, voice whispered within me,
"How can it not be?"

When Doubt and Travail my course pursue,
And in the midst of sorrow I ask, "How can it be?"
Then is the time I must be patient and strong,
Recognizing life's frailties,
And again recall that inner voice which asked,
"How can it not be?"

When Joy and Triumph present their gifts,
And in humility I ask, "How can it be?"
Then let me not forget those quiet words,
"How can it not be?"

For if I go hand-in-hand with the Lord,
Wherever the road may lead,
There is no need to ask, "How can it be?"
For He is with me to reassure,
"How can it not be?"

I don't presume to understand all the mysteries of the church. Nor do I understand how it was that a little boy from Kansas and a little girl from Idaho met, married, and were given a blessed life together. I don't understand how we 'found' our dream house in Lake Elsinore or why, exactly, I ended up living in a condo in San Clemente. I only understand I am grateful for the life I have had, and I believe in a personal God whom I try to love and serve, not only in the Church, but beyond the Church.

Beyond the confines of church walls, I also find my faith in God reinforced. I find it in the incredible love of my family. I am so blessed with children, grandchildren, and great-grandchildren. For almost fifty years I was blessed with the love of a husband, truly dear and good. Although, earlier, I might have thought it was I who brought him closer to God, I've come to see that we were spiritual partners as well as earthly partners, and without him at my side, I might not have grown into the fuller faith I now have.

Many people have sought to console me over the death of my son, Leon, this summer. I do miss him, his weekly phone calls, and his willingness to come in a heartbeat to help me if I needed it. I feel sorrow that his grandchildren will not remember his kindness, the joy they gave him, and his great love for them and their parents. But I also trust that God had better plans for him this summer, and I feel assured that, in time, we will be together again.

I should be remiss not to mention, once again, the kindness of friends as a gift from God. Together with my family, their comfort and companionship have given meaning to my life, especially since my husband died.

For example, in 2005, two years after my husband passed away, a friend asked me to accompany her on an Elderhostel excursion to Iceland and Greenland, two of the few places in the world which she had not visited. The trip was titled "On the Trail of the Vikings," and we learned that the Vikings made their way to North America via Iceland and Greenland for the purpose of converting, or *Christianizing,* as they put it, the pagans. On rocky hillsides, little was left to remind us of their efforts to bring their God to the people of this strange land. In my sketchbook, depicting a large circle of various sized stones, I wrote: *Only the stones are left, lying in rows, or scattered upon the landscape. Only the stones are left to tell the stories of struggle, of love, of triumph, of grief. Only the stones are left, markers of a bygone time.*

This past fall I joined a group of watercolor artists in Greece for three weeks of sight-seeing and painting. We first visited the area of Meteora, inland and north of Athens, where over eight hundred tall stone pinnacles rise up from the ground like a stone forest. On the tops of several of these rock formations are six Greek Orthodox monasteries built of stone hundreds of years ago. The literature told us it took over twenty years to haul all the stones up the perpendicular sides of the rocks before being fashioned into houses of worship.

Here again I was called by the stones. I wrote about one of these monasteries: *Tributes to an unseen God, as stone upon stone upon stone, the faithful build their walls high upon the peak, reaching heavenward, ever searching.*

Farther south on this trip, we were among the brilliant white and blue buildings and churches of the Cyclades Islands and the blue-green Aegean Sea that laps at their rocky beaches. On the small island of Delos, we walked among the ochre-colored stones, reminders of temples and walls and strange gods whom they worshiped. In Athens, we climbed the Acropolis and sketched the Parthenon, another tribute to their gods. All these were the settings for humans who lived thousands of years earlier.

And so it is that in every era, through all the generations, we have sought to find answers to our questions.

Ultimately, we rely on faith. And love.

Faith and love give meaning to my life.

Chapter 20 ...by a Backward Glance

To be truthful, it's a little scary, as I sit in my office/art room on this last month of the year, the year I saw my eightieth birthday, writing this last chapter of my life's story, as I have defined it. A little voice in the back of my head keeps asking, *What will people think when they read this? Am I sharing too much?* It's a little like walking in the emperor's new clothes. I have to admit it has taken courage, especially in the last few chapters, to declare my beliefs and my faith.

Actually, this isn't really the last chapter of my story. The last chapter will not be written by me. It will be spoken in the words of my family and friends. And again, the little voice asks, *What will they say? Should I worry about it?*

Getting beyond self-doubt, I must say I feel very fortunate, no, *blessed* is a better word, to have been able to look back over the years, even into the years before my birth. I have been able to paint word pictures of myself and my family. However, like any artist, these words come from my own interpretation of the lives of those who have been so much a part of me. Others may paint a different picture. But the little voice also says, *You can't worry about that. Remember, this is your life, as* you *see it.* Easy to say, but harder to accept.

If I were to define, or compartmentalize, the phases of my life, they would fall into five categories: my ancestry, my birth through the Philippine years, the Idaho years, married life, and widowhood. Each period has left an indelible mark.

Walt Whitman's words from *"There Was a Child Went Forth"* keep coming back to me:

> *There was a child went forth every day;*
> *And the first object he look'd upon,*
> *that object he became;*
> *And that object became part of him for the day,*
> *or a certain part of the day, or for many years,*
> *or stretching cycles of years.*

Although I never knew either of my grandfathers, thanks to the research of my sister-in-law, Connie Crawford, and the gleaning of information from several cousins, I was able to piece together a somewhat faint, I'll admit, picture of these men and their lives. Of my grandmothers, I painted the pictures from memories of the intermittent times I visited with them, read letters they had written, and stories that were told to me. Both of these women were hard-working and beloved by their children.

From personal correspondence, letters my father wrote to Catherine, and letters that she wrote to her mother, I learned about my parents' young adult years. The admirable characteristics of both parents were apparent as I read their histories with a backward glance.

When strangers or friends, learn that my early years were spent in the Philippine Islands during World War II, they are intrigued. "Really?" they ask. "Tell me about it. You should write a book." And so I have.

Pauline Crawford Crabb

Although I have often said the years of WWII were not the defining years of my life, I see now that the hardships imposed upon my family and me, did, in fact, have a tremendous impact on my life. One piece of evidence of that experience is my reaction to low flying helicopters and small planes. Although not always, but often, I recall the sounds of those American planes which flew over Santo Tomas on bombing raids during my time there, just as my senses also heighten, here in San Clemente, when the reverberations of heavy artillery being fired at the Marine Base on Camp Pendleton, a few miles away, reach my ear.

I see how the strength of my father, as he led us away from the comfortable life we had known, and the risks he took to keep his family safe, made their mark on me. Throughout his life, by example, he demonstrated the importance of integrity, and being true to one's own standards. His expectations of me have been lasting. "For God's sake, Mike, don't be a sheep," and "If I haven't taught you right from wrong by the time you're sixteen, it's too late," he had said. I didn't always succeed in living up to his expectations, but I never forgot his admonitions.

I know I've also been sculpted by the steadfastness of my mother as she raised five children. Her frugality is legend in the family. She loved to read, sew and do needlework. She valued education. She also inspired me by her strong faith.

While neither of my parents was long on accolades, I always knew, without a doubt, they loved me very much.

My ten Idaho years, only the blink of an eye in my overall life, found me identifying myself as a miner's daughter, the little girl from Idaho, who grew up and went to college. I wasn't as studious as my mother, but I did graduate, an opportunity lost to both my parents and grandparents.

I found the love of my life, Leon Dee Crabb, in college, married him after an eight-month courtship, and moved to California after a short hiatus in Las Vegas, Nevada. We raised three children, all of whom attended and graduated from college. As Leon and I recounted our blessings on the evening of our twenty-fifth wedding anniversary, we listed that fact, among many others, as something which gave us great satisfaction. I must also add, twenty-five years later, each of our children gave us two grandchildren, who now light up my life, and add another layer of richness as I have watched them grow into good and beautiful young men and women. They bring me much joy.

The three little girls who are my great-granddaughters now add to the joy I feel when I see them, or hear their parents speak of them in loving tones. I wonder what life will be like for them when they are my age.

As our chickadees grew up and left the nest, Leon and I enjoyed our life together. It would be foolish to write that we never had any problems to solve. We did, but we worked them out together. We worked hard, played hard, and prayed hard. We traveled widely, as often as we could with the Golden Eagle Jazz Band, and at other times by ourselves.

After we both retired, we moved to a new community, and made a new life there. When Leon became ill, I cared for him. In notes, written a month after his death, I said, *"...in his final days he often told me how much he appreciated the care I was giving him...It was care given with love and lovingly received."*

At sixty-nine and a half years of age, not by choice, I became truly independent. For the first time in my life, I was responsible to no one but myself. It was not always easy. Writing became a way of working through all the new experiences thrust upon me. One evening I wrote, *"It's just so darned weird, this feeling I have. Like it's not real. Life's not real anymore."* A few paragraphs later I wrote, *"I hope that someday I'll get used to this. I know I will. I have faith that the Lord will lead me in the right direction. Thank God for my faith."*

One year later, almost to the day, I wrote, *"I think I have done a good job this year, keeping our—now my—financial affairs in order..."* We had always been partners in our financial dealings, but now there were decisions I had to make on my own.

One of the biggest decisions, and the one which led to my current lifestyle, was selling my house in Tuscany Hills and moving to San Clemente. As I have written, it was traumatic at first, but, in retrospect, a good decision on my part. Living near the ocean brings me peace.

One day, not too long ago, after a session of plein air painting a scene of the San Clemente beach and the pier, these few words of *haiku* came to me:

Waves ~ tides ~ birds on wing
Flowing ~ breaking ~ gliding
Life's rhythms uninterrupted

At eighty, I have seen the rhythms of life, never ending, always flowing and ebbing. Sometimes they have brought joy, at other times great sorrow. Although my faith has always been strong, it is here in San Clemente, I believe, I have matured in that faith which brings me comfort. Sharing my faith with others in my church also gives me purpose. It nurtures me.

Many years ago, I was given a little ceramic knick-knack which sat above the kitchen sink in our home in Pasadena. Now, in San Clemente, it still sits on a counter above my sink where I can ponder its message as I'm doing dishes or cleaning up. Not more than three or four inches high, it's a little bald-pated Franciscan friar, holding an artist's brush, standing in front of an easel upon which he has painted these words:

"Peace Prayer"
Lord, make me an instrument of your peace.
Where there is hatred, let me sow your love;
where they is injury, pardon;
where there is doubt, faith;
where there is despair, hope;
where there is darkness, light
....and where there is sadness, joy.

The second verse of this well-known prayer (attributed to St. Francis of Assisi, but actually written in the early twentieth century) is equally poignant for me:

O Divine Master, Grant that I may not so much seek
To be consoled as to console;
To be understood as to understand;
To be loved as to love.
For it is in giving that we receive;
It is in pardoning that we are pardoned;
And it is in dying that we are born to eternal life.

Just think what I have to look forward to!

Chapter 21 ...I Returned

General Douglas MacArthur, with a salute of an upturned arm, famously announced, "I shall return!" as he left the Philippine island of Corregidor for Australia, shortly after the onset of World War II in the Pacific.

Paraphrasing General MacArthur, "I did return" to the Philippine Islands in February, 2015, seventy years after I had left.

Just when I think life is slowing down for me, another adventure beckons, and I can't say, "No." Some opportunities you just can't put off. They come around only once. This was one of those times. As I was in the process of writing my memoir, I was put in contact with a man who was also a civilian prisoner of war in Manila, on the island of Luzon, where my family and I were held prisoners during World War II. Through him, and an organization called BACEPOW (Bay Area Civilian Ex-Prisoners of War), I learned of a twelve-day tour to the Philippines to commemorate the seventieth anniversary of the liberation of Manila in February, 1945. More specifically, a ceremony was to be held at the University of Santo Tomas, on February 3, 2015, seventy years to the day when members of the United States 1st Cavalry Division tanks rammed down the front gates of the university to liberate over 3,500 internees of the Santo Tomas Internment Camp. Among these prisoners, were my family and I who had been held for two and a half years during the war.

I wrote about those years in an earlier chapter in this book, but neither I nor any others in my family had returned to the islands since our departure in April 1945. I thought this would be a great opportunity to bring more clarity to that period of my life, especially because it had, and continues to have, so great an effect on my life's perspectives. I didn't know how much I would remember.

What did I expect? Would I have any fear, trauma, or unexpected memories pop up to the surface when I walked through those iron gates where I might have died of starvation had we not been rescued so many years before? Would I meet people who knew my parents? What did I hope for? I didn't know and didn't spend much time thinking about what *might* happen. Of one thing I was quite sure: I didn't want to miss out on such an adventure.

I called my sister, Sharon, who lives in Spokane, Washington, and my brother, Don, who lives in northern California, to see if either one of them was interested in going. Sharon's family urged her to go. Don said he was not well enough to make the trip.

A few days later, Sharon emailed me to ask if I had any objections to her granddaughter, Alexandra, coming along with us.

"The more the merrier," I wrote back.

* * * * *

In this spirit of adventure, I made arrangements to meet Sharon and Alexandra in Oakland, where we would spend the night with Sharon's son, Bryan. Late on the afternoon of January thirtieth, we took a cab to the San Francisco International Airport for our long flight to Manila.

As we approached the check-in counter, we were greeted by our tour guides with the requisite ID tags, and complementary travel bags attesting to our group's purpose. I looked at the tags of others in our vicinity, perhaps thirty or forty people I reckoned. I hoped to recognize a familiar name I'd seen penciled in my father's handwriting, as he listed the names of those Americans who worked at the Itogon mine at the start of the war in a small notebook. None jumped out at me.

Mother had kept in touch with several families after the war. Would any of these people's names appear on a lanyard hung around the neck of some grey-haired traveler? No luck.

Certainly, I didn't expect to recognize any familiar faces. Seventy years had gone by since I might have been in the company of these travelers. I observed several intergenerational groups, perhaps children or grandchildren of former internees, but they were all strangers to me.

The ten-hour flight was routine and comfortable. I have no trouble sleeping on planes. We crossed the International Date Line, and I tried to calculate what day and hour it would be at home so I wouldn't interrupt my children's sleep with my "Arrived safely" phone message. I took the adventure in stride: tickets, passports, baggage claims, luggage checks.

* * * * *

We arrived in Manila in the pre-dawn hours of February first. Upon deplaning, the usual tourist procedures ensued: standing in line to show our passports at the customs' window, claiming luggage, looking for a person standing with a printed sign.

Once we spied a smiling middle-aged Filipino holding up the magic words *Manila Liberation Tour*, we followed him out the doors to a big yellow bus in the parking lot. Everyone gave a sigh of relief once we were seated, and Carlos, our guide for the next ten days, welcomed us. We were on our way to our home-away-from-home for the next few days.

It wasn't until our tour bus pulled up to the covered entrance of the Manila Hotel that my heart truly began skipping beats. Here was a setting in which my parents must have stayed in the days before the war. I might even have stayed here when Mother and I arrived on the *Tatsuta Maru.* It had berthed in Manila Harbor. Daddy had been there to meet us as we came down the gangplank, early in 1937.

As our group left the bus, we were met by beautifully garbed greeters who welcomed us to the hotel. I walked into a gaily colored lobby, decorated with red paper lanterns in preparation for the upcoming Chinese New Year, and imagined my parents, as a young couple, enjoying an evening cocktail in one of the bars just a stone's throw from the registration desk. Had they listened to musicians playing the popular music of the day? My head swirled, taking in a setting right from a movie set. I was excited.

* * *

Opened in 1912, the Manila Hotel was built to rival the Malancañang Palace, official residence of the president of the Philippines. As Military Advisor of the Philippine Commonwealth, General Douglas MacArthur occupied the luxurious penthouse for six years. During WWII, the hotel was almost totally destroyed, first by the Japanese, and then by the Americans. Since renovated, the penthouse, we were told, can be rented for $3,000 a night, complete with butler.

While our group waited for room assignments, we were given a tour of the MacArthur Suite, as the penthouse is named.

This was a totally different experience from the last time I had spent a night in Manila, seventy years before. My parents must have spent many restless hours as they lay on hard cots in our shanty near the outer wall of the Santo Tomas Interment Camp, first wondering if we would make it out alive, and later, in March, 1945, anticipating our departure for the island of Leyte, a first stop before returning to the United States. So much had happened in those intervening years.

* * * * *

Day Two dawned brightly. I drew back the drapes to take in the view from our eighth floor room.

I spotted the largest oil tanker I could ever imagine just a stone's throw from the hotel, berthed dockside in the bay. It appeared to be three or four stories high. To my left I saw the windows of the MacArthur penthouse.

"What will today bring?" I wondered.

Rajah Tours had planned each day full to the brim. This day was no exception. We were to be ready to be on the bus for Corregidor Island by seven o'clock in order to take an early ferry across the twenty-six miles to the site of MacArthur's last stand in the Philippines. In as short a time as it takes three women to get ready for a day's adventure, we hopped to it, not wanting to leave without breakfast.

Over the years, I've started my day at many a hotel buffet breakfast, but I was not prepared for the variety of cultural cuisines offered by the Manila Hotel. Asian, European, English, American, you-name-it, and there was a food station dishing up the specialty of your desire. None of my morning meals eaten in the hotel could be called run-of-the-mill. I took advantage of the great variety of food and beverages, and savored each one.

The view meeting us in the small harbor as our group disembarked from the ferry was a typical tropical scene with lush greenery and tall coconut trees. But as our group, riding in an open-sided tram, came across the skeletons of the barracks where United States military men had lived and died seventy-three years ago, the tour began to take on a more somber aspect. It reminded us of the reason we'd come on this journey.

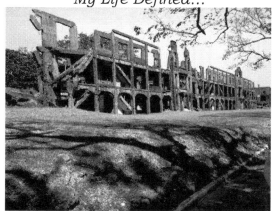

The barracks' shells of concrete, constructed in 1921 and destroyed in 1942, keep memories of the horrific loss of lives, both American and Filipino. In close proximity to the barracks are several canons used first by the Americans against the Japanese invaders. They were disabled before the surrender of May 6, 1942, but put back into action by American POWs. They were finally put out of commission by US bombs in January, 1945.

A silent group walked back to our tram for the short ride from the old barracks to the Malinta Tunnel, used as headquarters for the Americans and Filipinos prior to the surrender of the island. For the younger generation who had no first-hand knowledge of the Battle of Corregidor, and for those of us old enough to have forgotten most of the details, this memorial site, through dioramas

251

projected from several side tunnels, tells the story of the
time, the place, and the people who fought for freedom
from oppression.

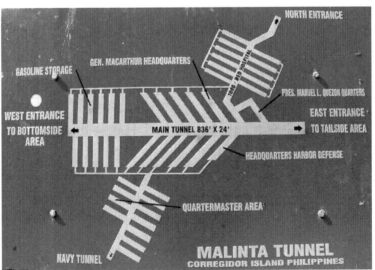

For the historians on the tour, beyond the Malinta
Tunnel stands a concrete wall listing every battle of the
Pacific Theater, and a museum with its maps and

memorabilia. All this provides further concrete evidence of the magnitude of destruction of World War II in this small part of the world.

Photos of the Bataan Death March were stark reminders of how many gave their lives fighting for freedom. As Edmund Burke (and many others, in so many words) said, "Those who don't know history are doomed to repeat it." It was good to be reminded.

Personally, I found the Flame of Freedom and the Dome of Light touched my heart most profoundly. Each, in its own way, speaks to the dignity of every human being. War has a way of denying that reality

TO LIVE IN FREEDOM'S LIGHT
IS THE RIGHT OF MANKIND

**SLEEP MY SON, YOUR DUTY DONE
FOR FREEDOM'S LIGHT HAS COME
SLEEP IN THE SILENT DEPTH OF THE SEA
OR IN YOUR BED OF HALLOWED SOD
UNTIL YOU HEAR AT DAWN
THE LOW CLEAR REVEILEE OF GOD.**

Following a side trip to see the dock from which General MacArthur left the island, with his famous quote: "I shall return," and several other locales with reminders of WWII, our group was treated to a buffet luncheon.

After plenty of time for photos, we hopped aboard our tram and were driven back to the ferry. It was a quieter group who returned to Manila.

* * *

Anticipation, along with a bit of anxiety, built up in me as I began wondering what tomorrow would bring. The following day, February third, marked the seventieth anniversary of the liberation of Santo Tomas by the First Cavalry Division of the United States Army. A reception was planned for the returning internees on the campus of Santo Tomas University.

Another early departure from the hotel was scheduled, but neither Sharon, Alexandra nor I wanted to miss the chance for another delicious breakfast there. The evening before, I laid out my outfit: light beige pants with a red vest over a blue and white shirt. Without actually waving a flag, I wanted to be as patriotic as possible to Old Glory.

Carlos greeted us shortly before seven-thirty as our group boarded two awaiting busses. We made our way through the streets of Manila until we came to the tall archway, which marked the entrance to Santo Tomas University. The Main Building seemed very familiar to me as it loomed ahead. Whether I remembered it from my experiences there, or from pictures I'd seen doing my research, I can't say.

As I climbed down from the bus, I surveyed the grounds around us. Standing apart from a shaded area with concrete benches, we saw three uniformed soldiers. Each wore a different uniform of WWII vintage. As I looked at the soldier in the middle of the trio, an uncomfortable tension rose inside of me. I immediately recognized him as representing a Japanese soldier.

The uniforms of the other two soldiers represented the United States and the Philippines. Remembering my father's experiences during the war made it hard for me to feel at ease. Intellectually, I think I understood the reasoning for having representatives from all three armies, but emotionally I reverted to an earlier time so many, many years ago.

We were given time to mull around the plaza in front of the Main Building. I wondered if this was the place where I'd practiced my handstands and backbends when we first came into Santo Tomas. A number of the internees opted to have their photos taken with the uniformed men. Refugio, the photographer who accompanied our tour, took pictures for the annals of history. First, only we internees posed in front of the building, and then he included our entire group in another photo.

Shortly afterward, we were ushered through the entrance doors into the foyer of the building. Colorful murals, representing historical figures of the university, filled the walls. Each of us signed in, and then made our way over to long tables lined with delicious edibles and beverages. On the other side of the foyer, a podium stood in front of several rows of chairs, set up for the occasion. A heavy red, white, and blue ribbon with a large red, white, and blue bow was strung across the Philippine mahogany stairway leading to the upper floors.

Once we were all seated, a representative of the university welcomed us and outlined the short program of events for the occasion. One member of our group, Sascha Jansen, responded on behalf of our group, and expressed our appreciation for the efforts made by the university to make the occasion memorable for us.

Following this, we all lined up on the staircase, which some of us had climbed so many years ago. More photos were taken. I seemed to have watched the entire ceremony more from the viewpoint of an observer, rather than one who had actually participated in the events being talked about. It evoked only a mildly emotional response in me, although I was glad I was able to be a part of this historic moment.

* * * * *

As the formal program came to an end, we were given a couple of options: we could see a relevant movie in the little theater, or we could attend a meeting of former internees with a chance to tell our stories, to add our oral histories to the archives of the university. The Crawford clan decided we would like to hear the stories of our fellow internees.

Young students attending the university, some of whom might be learning about this part of the university's role in WWII for the first time, had also been invited to be observers.

Brightly colored murals depicting the history of the university covered the walls of our meeting room. Before the oral history telling began, we were served another buffet luncheon, and given time to chat among ourselves. Then, for an hour or so following lunch, Maita Oebanda, Collection Management and Documentation Assistant, and curator of the Museum of Arts and Sciences at STU, facilitated our telling of personal experiences during the war.

Representing the Crawford family, I got up and told of our eleven months in the mountains of Luzon before we surrendered to the Japanese. I don't recall being overly emotional while I related our tale. And I don't recall being very emotional as I heard the stories of other internees.

Following our oral history session, one of the former internees, using a seventy-year-old map of the 1945 campus, led those of us who were interested on a tour of the university grounds. We gathered around our guide, trying to imagine where we were seventy years ago. Students walked among us, to and from classes. Some sat on cement benches studying, generally having a good time with their fellow classmates. Cars came and went by roads, which were non-existent when we were there.

Without our guide having the benefit of a microphone, I had a hard time hearing and couldn't put myself back into the WWII setting. I couldn't picture our little shanty, or the pathways I took to bring our meals back from a chow line. Those memories must be hidden under many other layers of memories I've created in the past seventy years.

Before leaving the Santo Tomas University campus, Sharon, Alexandra, and I walked up to the floor which houses the STU museum. An entire area is dedicated to an exhibit of artifacts from the STIC era. Prominently displayed on a wall plaque is the rationale for the evidence of memories created by the WWII internees. It reads:

> *The legacy of faith and fortitude left by the internees' three-year experience burns like a bright beacon for a new generation. Our task is to learn from their story, so that we may guard against the mistakes that cost all humanity a price too dear to ever pay.*

I was thrilled to find my family's names listed on another plaque naming all the internees in the camp. Here was the connection I'd been looking for. Here was the proof we had been through this profound experience—my father, my mother, my sister, my brother

258

and I. Until I read with my own eyes the names: Paul Rexford Crawford, Catherine Crawford, Pauline Shirley Crawford, Sharon Lee Crawford, and Donald Ladd Crawford, I might as well have been in any historical museum, viewing, with only an abstract interest, the history presented before me.

Seeing this plaque made up for the lack of finding a connection between my family and any of the other visitors on this tour. Perhaps this moment was the reason I was meant to return.

By late afternoon, my sister, my great-niece, and I had wandered around the campus, taken pictures from every possible vista, and were more than ready to take our leave. When we spied our bus, ready for the return to the Manila Hotel, I walked down the brick path, which leads into the campus, took a last photo of the statue of St. Thomas Aquinas, right arm extended over the campus as if blessing the university and those of us who had returned.

I accepted the blessing and realized this would most likely be the last time I would return to the Philippines.

We headed toward the bus and found our seats. As we passed through the gates of the university, making our way onto the main road, I glanced back and felt a little melancholy, as though I were leaving the ghosts of the past behind.

Another delicious dinner of Filipino and Chinese cuisine awaited us in one of the hotel's dining rooms. Again, we were seated with a group of strangers, some of them also descendants of the internees. I recall no deep discussions, nor did we share other poignant memories. Our present interest in the meal took precedence over re-hashing the past.

* * * * *

The next morning, as we prepared for another day's adventure, Sharon decided she would stay back at the hotel while the rest of us boarded the bus for the day's tour. She had been feeling poorly the day before and felt she needed the rest.

Carlos, our guide, again warmly welcomed us as we boarded our Raja Tour bus. Taxis, buses, and bicycles of every description wove in and out of our path as we wended our way through the hectic early morning traffic. I was reminded of the chaotic street scenes I'd experienced in India a few years earlier.

Our first stop took us to a broad green expanse of a park honoring the first president of the Philippines, Jose Rizal. It was he who protested against the treatment of his country by the Spaniards, and was assassinated in 1895, becoming a national hero. We would see another tribute to this man while we were in the Intromuros, a walled compound within the city of Manila.

For most of my life, I believed when Santo Tomas Internment Camp was liberated on February 3, 1945, the Japanese army had been defeated. Far from it. A terrible battle raged for almost a month, and over 100,000 people lost their lives during that time.

We were later told that outside of Warsaw, Poland, Manila was the city most devastated by the bombings and other horrors of World War II. As we drove through the streets in the poorer areas of the city, we could see the truth of this statement. Much of the area still looked war-torn after these seventy years. Many cement block buildings appeared charred, and electric wires hung precariously across alleys. Other sections of the city contain modern skyscrapers and shopping malls, but remnants of battle remain.

Within the next few kilometers, we came to another reminder of the war: the Memorare Manila Monument.

Sitting atop a huge black marble base, the sculpted figure of a woman sits, holding a small infant in her arms. Four other figures of varying ages, lie about her in various postures of recline.

An inscription on the base of the marble reads:
MEMORARE - MANILA 1945
THIS MEMORIAL IS DEDICATED TO ALL THOSE
INNOCENT VICTIMS OF WAR. MANY OF WHOM WENT
NAMELESS AND UNKNOWN TO A COMMON GRAVE, OR
NEVER EVEN KNEW A GRAVE AT ALL, THEIR BODIES
HAVING BEEN CONSUMED BY FIRE OR CRUSHED TO
DUST BENEATH THE RUBBLE OF RUINS.
LET THIS MONUMENT BE A GRAVESTONE FOR EACH
AND EVERY ONE OF THE OVER 100,000 MEN, WOMEN,
CHILDREN AND INFANTS KILLED IN MANILA DURING ITS
BATTLE OF LIBERATION – FEBRUARY 3 – MARCH 3,
1945. WE HAVE NOT FORGOTTEN THEM. NOR SHALL
WE EVER FORGET.
MAY THEY REST IN PEACE AS PART NOW OF THE
SACRED GROUND OF THIS CITY: THE MANILA OF OUR
AFFECTIONS.
FEBRUARY 18,1995

When we reached the Intromuros, which was used as a prison for Filipinos during WWII, we saw more evidence of the terrible vicissitudes of war and man's inhumanity toward fellow man. I choose not to elaborate on the details of such cruel treatment of the prisoners. It is enough to say each stop was a poignant reminder of the cost of war on civilians as well as military personnel.

Interspersing these somber experiences with rewards of culinary delights helped soften the weight of the devastating reminders of the past. At noon, we enjoyed another delicious buffet at the Ilustrado Restaurant in downtown Manila, after which we were driven a short distance to the American Cemetery for a wreath-laying ceremony.

* * * * *

Another sobering sight met our eyes as we entered the grounds of the American Cemetery. Tall buildings in the distance, marking signs of modern architecture in Manila, dwarfed the 17,206 white crosses marking the graves of 16,636 Americans and 570 Filipinos who perished in the war. The American Battle Monument Commission continues to maintain the cemetery.

Each person's name is engraved on one of the walls that encircle a small chapel on the grounds. A large wreath of yellow, white, pink and deep lavender flowers, with a sash reading *The Price for Freedom* stood on an easel at the entrance to the chapel as our group gathered around for a short ceremony conducted by one of the retired American military personnel. We were free to wander about the small museum on the grounds or to request to be taken to a particular gravesite if we wished to pay our respects to the person buried there.

I asked to be shown the graves of four men who were shot by the Japanese trying to escape from STIC. At least one of these men had worked under my father at the

Itogon mine, and I had seen the names of all four written in the small notebook my father kept while we were captives.

In retrospect, I know I was looking for as many connections with my father (my dad, my Daddy) as I could find.

My hopes were fulfilled here, as a guide picked me up in a little shuttle and drove us to the area where these men were buried. I took photos of the four white crosses, lined in a row among the field of thousands of others, who lost their lives as the price of freedom. They have not been forgotten.

* * * * *

Remembering the fallen at the cemetery marked the final tribute our little band of ex-POWs paid to the memory of our WWII experiences.

I think of the following day, February fifth, as the beginning of our trip as regular *oohing* and *aahing* tourists who enjoyed the sights of a new country.

We were taken to the Villa Escudero, some distance from Manila, where we enjoyed riding on a *carabao*-pulled cart, swimming or canoeing in a small manmade lake, or wandering through the shocking pink building, which housed a museum. Sharon, Alexandra and I opted for the water sport. We paddled a raft and swam in a warm pool.

That evening, Alexandra became quite ill with a high fever, as well as the other usual symptoms often experienced by tourists. The medical staff at the hotel couldn't have been more conscientious, and made several trips to our room to see after Alexandra's welfare. When morning came, I decided to stay with her while Sharon joined the group touring Makati City and its shopping attractions.

Luckily, the following day was Sunday, with nothing formal planned. Alexandra felt better, but Sharon and I decided it would be a good day to keep a low profile. Several of our group hired a bus and were driven to Los Baños, an hour or so away. Some of them, including my new friend, Gerry Ann Schwede, had been interned there. We declined to join them, and spent some time lolling around the pool, enjoying a drink, and tasting more delicious food.

* * * * *

February ninth was a bittersweet day as we bade farewell to Manila and the Manila Hotel. I was sad to be leaving, but our tour took us farther out into the countryside.

I thought perhaps here I might find a sense of belonging, a bringing to light more memories from my childhood. I was not disappointed.

With Carlos in the front seat across from the bus driver, we received a running commentary of what the day would bring. The landscape of funky taxis, broken-down wires, and burnt-out buildings, left me wondering how these people survived.

The city gradually gave way to wide-open vistas of greenery, of banana and coconut palm trees. We even passed one vividly colored building complex, which reminded me of a Disney attraction.

The moment we stopped at a small fruit stand along the side of the road, miles out of the city, I began to recall snippets of my past. I recognized bunches of varied-sized bananas hanging from its thatched roof. Some of the bananas were so small I could cup one in the palm of my hand. I've never seen these in the States. I also saw large jackfruit, *lanzones*, and guavas, as well as other fruits unfamiliar to me.

Before long, in the distance, loomed the dormant Taal volcano crater. Although quiet now, it has erupted several times over hundreds of years, the last time in 1977, with a substantial loss of life as lava, hot steam, and ashes rained down on the area. Now, in 2015, it seemed but a quiet reminder of the past. The blue sky, with scattered clouds hovering over small slate-blue lakes, brought on more *oohs* and *aahs* as our eyes scoured the landscape from the bus. Our overnight stay was to be at the Taal Vista Hotel in Tagatay City.

In the lobby of the hotel (much more modest than the Manila Hotel), our group was welcomed with a huge, round, outsized arrangement of rust, white and purple colored flowers, which looked like daisies or chrysanthemums, sitting atop a small round table. In front of the table, on a gold framed easel, stood the sign: "Celebrate Liberation 1945 Group – Sampaguita Ballroom – February 9, 2015."

In the ballroom, as we stood in line for yet another buffet lunch, we were serenaded by three guitarists playing tunes from the '20s, '30s, or '40s. They knew their audience. I recognized most of the melodies. It was good to have some leisure time to walk around the grounds of hotel and enjoy the lush green landscape with the volcano, small islands, and lakes in the distance. So peaceful.

But no long rest for tourists. After we located our rooms, we were herded back into the bus, and driven around the city of Taal, with a stop at the Minor Basilica of St. Martin of Tours, the largest church in the Philippine Islands. On its present site for over a hundred years, the church was last renovated fifty years ago. Besides its size and architecture, the main altar of bright silver dazzles the eye.

Before heading back to Manila after breakfast the next morning, we visited two other attractions in Taal: a church with an organ created from bamboo, and a museum of Sarao Jeepneys. Both were unique in their own way, and added to our enjoyment of the trip. Frosting on the cake, you might say. But this was our last day in the Philippines, and I became restless, thinking about the trip home.

* * * * *

The Sofitel Hotel, located near the airport, was our home-away-from-home for our last night in the Philippines. In a brightly lit outdoor dining area, we enjoyed a barbecue dinner and were entertained by a troupe of performers in colorful costumes presenting their national dances. Some of our group were drawn into the festivities, taking turns on the dance floor. There were no speeches and no formal program signaling the end of the seventieth anniversary of liberation for the internees.

Before we said our goodnights, Gerry Ann Schwede and I exchanged addresses and phone numbers. She was the only person with whom I had made a connection to my parents, and only tangentially because she knew a man in the States who had worked at Itogon. Gerry now lives in central California, and we made plans to see each other at another BACEPOW (Bay Area Civilian Ex-Prisoners Of War) reunion, which was to be held in Sacramento in April.

On the long plane ride back to San Francisco, I had hours and hours to ponder my experiences of the previous eleven days. Interestingly, in retrospect, I don't remember feeling happy. I don't remember feeling sad. I do know I felt very disappointed because I had not met anyone who even knew my father or mother, let alone who was a friend of theirs. Perhaps, more than wanting to dredge up memories of my years in Santo Tomas, I went to try to create some connection to my parents. It did not happen.

What I did learn was my sister, Sharon, and I had very different memories of our time in the internment camp. She attributes this to being five years younger, and staying close to Mother, whereas I was older and went to school every day.

We also have treated our past very differently. I seem to have put those years and memories behind me, as if they were souvenirs to be placed in a box, tied with a ribbon, and stored away in the large steamer trunk, which sits in my bedroom. I've used them to write my story, but they are only a small part of who I am.

It's not that I'm not interested in my history. In April, 2015, following our trip to the Philippines, I drove to Sacramento where I met Sharon, who had flown from Spokane. My brother, Don, whose daughter, Katia, had driven him from their home in Janesville, California, also came for another BACEPOW 70th Anniversary of Liberation Reunion, held over a weekend at an Embassy Suites Hotel. This time my daughter, Mary, came as well.

Through speeches and filmed documentaries, I learned more of the historical background of the war for the liberation of the Philippines. Katia and Mary fit into the category of "descendants," and one session over the weekend was held just for them. They laughed and joked at the label *descendant*, but found the session enlightening. Its focus was on sharing ways their parents (or perhaps grandparents) have or had reacted to their experiences as POWs.

Mary told me vast differences existed among families. Some talked about it a great deal of the time; some not at all.

One common trait seemed to be an emphasis on saving things. "You might need this someday," many parents would say.

Another common admonition was, "Clean your plate. Don't waste food." I fall into that category. I still have a hard time throwing food away. Katia and Mary both said they felt they had a deeper understanding of their parents than before the meeting.

And, it was good for Don, Sharon, and me to have some time to spend together. We live hundreds of miles apart, and times of family gatherings come far and few between these years.

In August of the same year, still hoping to meet someone, anyone, who knew my parents, I went to yet another BACEPOW reunion. This meeting was in Long Beach, less than two hours from my home in San Clemente, and it was only a day-long program.

I was happy to see some familiar faces I'd met in the Philippines and in Sacramento, and to meet a few others who were new to me. One woman, Karen Lewis, and I have a mutual friend, and a mutual interest in art, which added to my pleasure.

One of the admonitions I heard at the meeting was, "We can't let them forget." I know it's important for historians to record the realities of wars: the victories, the defeats, the atrocities, and the kindnesses (as there are also those who have selflessly given of their lives for the benefit of others).

Other than writing this chapter because I think it brings closure to a past experience, I don't spend much time dwelling on that short period of my life.

I enjoyed the afternoon, but afterwards realized I do not need to keep searching for someone who might have known me or my parents so many years ago. As of the day I write this, my time spent in STIC was only .03219316 of my life, and the percentage keeps getting more minute with every breath I take.

However, that being said, because I live in a town close to a Marine base, I am apt, on the occasion when it seems appropriate, to approach a serviceman and say to him, "Thank you for serving. It was young men like you who saved me and my family many years ago during World War II when I was a civilian prisoner of war."

They almost always reply, "Thank you, ma'am." I hope this helps them realize they are appreciated.

* * * * *

I am very grateful I was able to return to the Philippines to participate in the Seventieth Liberation Anniversary celebration. I was a part of the history, and appreciate those who keep the historical records of the time. I am most thankful for being able to add this last chapter to my memoir. However, it's not the last chapter of my life. Someone else will write that one.

Who knows how many years, months, or even days, I have left in this world? I want to create new memories, not relive old ones. I want to spend more time being grateful for what I have today, and not remembering what I didn't have seventy-some years ago.

I am grateful I can walk out the front door of my condo and take in the salty ocean air. I'm grateful for the love of my family and friends, and for my faith in a loving God.

A blue-and-white striped coffee mug sits atop a shelf above my computer. On it is printed: "Every Day is an Adventure."

Amen.